Wisdom Is Supreme

Navigating Life with Wisdom
from the Book of Proverbs

Bert de Ruiter

ISBN 978-3-95776-167-5

Photo credits (Cover): Shutterstock

VTR Publications, Gogolstr. 33, 90475 Nürnberg, Germany,
info@vtr-online.com, http://www.vtr-online.com.

CONTENTS

CHAPTER 10
The Wise Man and His Spouse

CHAPTER 11
The Wise Man and His Lifestyle

CHAPTER 12
Conclusion: Wisdom Better than Gold?

Appendix
Background Information about the bBook of Proverbs

FOREWORD

"Ask for whatever you want me to give you …"

During a recent dinner with several colleagues, the question came up: "What is the nicest present you ever received?" Different answers were given. Several answers that struck me were: "A compliment when I was around ten years old" and "A box of Lego when I was 8 years old." Receiving presents, of whatever kind, can have an enormous impact on one's life. A present does not always have be large in economic terms, to be valued emotionally. Also, what a present is worth might also depend on how life enfolds further.

I guess all of us have, at one time or another in our lives, made a list of presents we would like to have, for example for our birthday, wedding, or another anniversary. Usually, around Christmas (or St. Nicolas day, the 5th of December in the Netherlands) children and adults make wish lists and receive presents in their shoe or under the Christmas tree.

Suppose one of the richest people in the world, for example Bill Gates, the co-founder of the software company Microsoft, whose net worth is more than \$ 88 billion, invites you to hand in your wish list to him with the words: "Ask for whatever you want me to give you." Knowing that his resources would be able to back up his promise, what would you request?

Your request will be more than just a five-euro present.

In this book I want to look at a person from the Bible who faced that decision, namely Solomon. Only in Solomon's case, the offer was made by the One who owns far more than the resources of the world's richest man. We read in the Bible: *"At Gibeon the LORD appeared to Solomon during the night in a dream, and God said, "Ask for whatever you want me to give you."*" (1 Kings 3:5)

Solomon was a young man, about twenty years of age, when his father David died, and he became king. A young man presented with the vast array of possibilities God's offer could have been tempted him in many different directions, yet he asked God for the most important thing he could think of. His answer to God was:

"… so, give your servant a discerning heart to govern your people and to distinguish between right and wrong …" (1 Kings 3:9)

In 2 Chronicles 1, the same story is written with slightly different words and the answer Solomon gives to the Lord's offer is: *"Give me wisdom and knowledge …"* (2 Chronical 1:10)

Would young men and women of twenty years old today give the same answer? Would we? Or would we prefer health, wealth, or fame?

We might say: "I want fame, because then I can tell everyone about you." Or: "I want a good health, so I can use all my time to live for you and do mighty works." Or: "I want wealth to provide the needs of so many in this world." Or: "I want power to influence the institutions around the world to do good instead of evil."

The One who owns everything there is and who is All-Powerful, offered Solomon everything and Solomon choose wisdom and a discerning heart.

This was an answer that pleased God and one that He was more than willing to grant, and He responded to Solomon: *"I will do what you have asked. I will give you a wise and discerning heart …"* (1 Kings 3:12)

Why did Solomon ask for wisdom instead of something else?

We get two clues when we read the context of the verses mentioned above.

First, Solomon acknowledged his need of wisdom because he admitted his own weakness and insufficiency for the task he had been given. Just prior to his request for wisdom, Solomon prays:

> Now, O Lord my God, you have made your servant king in place of David my father, but I am only a little child and do not know how to carry out my duties. Your servant is here among the people you have chosen, a great people, too numerous to count or number. (1 Kings 3:7,8)

He realizes that his responsibility for being king, in the footsteps of a successful king like his father David, exceeds his own resources. He is young, lacks experience, and is dealing with a large responsibility. In seeing this, he asks for wisdom.

We usually ask for things that we think we need. The reason many people today do not have wisdom high on their wish list is because we overestimate our own competencies. So often, we believe we have what it takes to live our live. If we are Christians, we might acknowledge we need God's help to complement our insufficiency in some areas of life, but we often find it hard to acknowledge our total bankruptcy.

The more we understand our own limits, our own weaknesses, our own insufficiencies, our own frailty, the more we cry out for wisdom and discernment.

The second reason that Solomon asked for wisdom, might be that the appreciation of wisdom had been installed in his heart from early childhood.

> Now you yourself know what Joab son of Zeruiah did to me – what he did to the two commanders of Israel's armies, Abner son of Ner, and Amasa son of Jether. He killed them, shedding their blood in peacetime as if in battle, and with that blood stained the belt around his waist and on the sandals on his feet. Deal **with him according to your wisdom**, but do not let his gray head go down to the grave in peace. But show kindness to the sons of Barzillai of Gilead and let them be among those who eat at your table. They stood by me when I fled from your brother Absalom. And remember, you have with you Shimei son of Gera, the Benjaminite from Bahurim, who called down bitter curses on me the day I went to Mahanaim. When he came down to meet me at the Jordan, I swore to him by the Lord: 'I will not put you to death by the sword.' But now, do not consider him innocent. You **are a man of wisdom;** you will know what to do to him. Bring his gray head down to the grave in blood." (1 Kings 2:5–9)

When David appointed Solomon as his successor and gave him some instructions, he refers to his wisdom and calls him a man of wisdom. David recognized that his son Solomon was a wise man even before Solomon asked God for wisdom! Solomon therefore wisely understood his need for the gift of wisdom to be given to him by God as he undertook the responsibilities of being Israel's king.

It takes a wise person to ask for wisdom. People that are less wise might have asked for strength to rule the kingdom, or riches, to help deal with the poor, or ...

God answered Solomon's prayer abundantly.

Whenever one asks who the wisest person in the Old Testament is, the answer invariably is: "Solomon". Solomon collected wisdom from the various cultures around Israel as well as from Israel itself, which he then filtered through the words of God's revelation. The wisdom that Solomon collected contained practical advice on how to live successfully considering God's words.

Although we do not run a kingdom, we need wisdom as much as Solomon did. We need the wisdom of God to navigate successfully through life. Like Solomon, we should ask God for wisdom. And like David, we should be teaching our families how valuable this commodity is.

The wisdom that Solomon received has found its way in the book called Proverbs that we find in the Bible today. In this book we find many short sayings, one-liners that expresses what life looks like when one is wise and what the consequences are when one lacks wisdom.

In the opening verses of the book of Proverbs Solomon explains what the main purpose of the book is and the effect the content of the book aims to have on the readers, namely: to teach us wisdom and understanding, and a disciplined and righteous life. The book is intended to make us into a mature person, in whose life the awe of God is the basis. The book aims to teach us the ability to live the way God wants us to, with an emotional intelligence, a character formed by the Word of God, and a way of living that exemplifies the righteousness of God.

It is to this book that I want to turn to in the pages that follow, in chapter 1 we learn about how the book of Proverbs encourages our quest for wisdom. In chapter 2, we discover that, even though the origin of the term 'wisdom' goes back to the beginning of human history, there still is no consensus about what we mean by 'wisdom.'

Also, gradually wisdom changed from being a divine virtue to being a human accomplishment, while in the book of Proverbs wisdom is the skill for living as God intends. In chapter 3, we learn about the concept of 'the fear of the LORD', which is both the foundation of and the result of wisdom. In chapter 4, the quest for wisdom is compared with digging for gold and we learn what are the necessary steps that we need to take in our quest for wisdom. We look at what suggestions the book of Proverbs gives us on how to become wise and seek to answer the questions, whether we become wiser when we get older and whether one can learn wisdom in a school. In chapter 5 we look at several key characteristics of a wise person, as defined by psychologists, philosophers as well as the book of Proverbs. In chapter 6 we look at the importance of diligence not only in acquiring wisdom, but also in using it our daily lives. In chapter 7 we discover that a wise person knows the proper values of wealth and uses it to honor God. In chapter 8 we learn that the words we speak reveal our wisdom or the lack of it. In chapters 9 and 10 we see that wisdom has an enormous impact on our relationships, particularly with our friends and our spouse. Chapter 11 points out the wisdom is not only about speaking wise words or doing wise things, but is a way of life. In chapter 12, the last chapter of the book we draw the lessons of the book to a close and learn that being wise is growing in an intimate relationship with the Creator and fashioning one live in accordance with the created order.

It is my desire that this book will encourage you to get wisdom and to continue to in becoming a wise person.

CHAPTER 1
THE QUEST FOR WISDOM:
MAN'S MOST BASIC DRIVE

Of all the pursuits open to men, the search for
wisdom is most perfect, more sublime, more
profitable, and more full of joy.
Thomas Aquinas

Among humankind one finds a quest to understand the meaning and purpose of life, a quest for the ultimate nature of reality and man's relationship to this reality. This is a quest for wisdom, it is an intellectual thirst to understand: to understand oneself, one's environment, the reason for one's existence, the problem of one's pain. This quest is a desire to grasp reality. The quest for wisdom begins with a desire to pursue it, to consider its worth, to see the benefit of it, to realize our need for it, and to awaken our desire for it. This quest for wisdom has been part of mankind from the beginning. It might even be considered man's most basic drive. Origen declared, "this desire, this longing to know the design of things has been implanted in us by God."[1]

Great thinkers of the past, such as Confucius, Socrates, Plato, and Aristotle have suggested that the pursuit of wisdom is the most noble and worthy human pursuit.

Also, King Solomon in the book of Proverbs emphasizes that seeking wisdom should be our life's priority.

A quest for wisdom is a quest to understand, to control, and to apprehend. It is a quest for meaning. But when this quest is undertaken, apart from God it becomes the foundation of sin.

When Satan tempted Eve in the Garden, he appealed to her quest for wisdom. He tempted her to eat of the tree of the knowledge of good and evil, saying: *"God knows when you eat of it your eyes will be opened, and you will be like God, knowing good and evil."* As a result, Eve had another look at the tree and she saw that *"the fruit of the tree was good for food and pleasing to the eye, and **also desirable for gaining wisdom** ..."* (Gen. 3:5,6)

---

[1]   Origin. *On First Principles*. (Notre Dame IN: Ave Maria Press Inc., 2013), 187.

There is nothing wrong with this quest for wisdom, provided it is done within the parameters set by the Sovereign Creator of the universe and under His authority.

But whenever this quest is undertaken in a way that ignores and bypasses God, we run into trouble. When our quest for wisdom comes from a desire to be like God and to live life independently from God, we will end up being called 'fools.' Eve's quest for wisdom let to her and consequently mankind's downfall: the relationship between man and God, between man and man and between man and the rest of creation was broken and paradise was lost.

> *The bid that Adam and Eve took to gain autonomous wisdom is shown to be foolish and to carry tragic, though not irremediable, consequences.*[2]

Our quest for wisdom, our desire to understand reality, therefore needs to begin with the acknowledgment of the absolute sovereignty of the Creator.

> *The search for knowledge can go wrong because of one single mistake at the beginning. One becomes competent and expert as far as the orders of life are concerned only if one begins from knowledge about God …*[3]

Within these parameters we are free to explore, to pursue wisdom, to look for it, to look out for it and to welcome it, even when it comes to us through human philosophy and non-Christian religions.

The book of Proverbs encourages us to embark on this quest for wisdom in three ways:

a. Wisdom is commended as something of the utmost value.

b. Those that have experienced this value of wisdom encourage us to acquire wisdom.

c. Wisdom herself invites us to come to her.

Wisdom is commended as something of the utmost value

Blessed are those who find wisdom, those who gain understanding, for she is more profitable than silver and yields better returns than gold. She is more precious than rubies; nothing you desire can compare with her. Long life is in

---

[2]   Sinclair, Maurice W. *Pathways of Wisdom: Human philosophies and the purpose of God* (Nottingham: Apollos, 2010), 23.

[3]   Gerard von Rad, *Wisdom in Israel*, (London, SCM Press, 1972), 67.

her right hand; in her left hand are riches and honor. Her ways are pleasant ways, and all her paths are peace. She is a tree of life to those who take hold of her; those who hold her fast will be blessed. (Proverbs 3:13–18)[4]

Those who find wisdom are considered models to be envied and imitated, they are commended and are considered happy people, because wisdom provides all that money and wealth cannot buy: real and everlasting life. Life as the Creator has intended it: peaceful, pleasant, productive, and secure. Life in close fellowship with Him. This is what humanity lost in Paradise, when because of sin the Lord closed their access to the Tree of Life.

> Proverbs functions symbolically (and provisionally) as the "tree of life that was lost in Genesis 2:22–24. By including this metaphor with some prominence, the author makes clear that until we reach 'the tree of life, which is in the paradise of God' (Revelation 2:7), we hold fast to the life-giving wisdom of the book of Proverbs and, more importantly, to Jesus Christ, who supersedes Solomon's wisdom."[5]

Humanity has tried to build a road back to this Tree of Life ever since, through religion, sacrifices, good works, and self-flagellation. But it can only be found back by holding on to God's wisdom, because, as we will see, wisdom is the fruit that grows from the attitude of the fear of the Lord. Such fear encompasses both awesomeness and intimacy with the One who created the universe and all that is in it. He created and sustained the world through wisdom and when we submit our life to His authority will we begin to live in harmony with Him and with the created order and begin to develop that same wisdom in our own lives.

> "If the Lord with wisdom as his tool accomplished the wonders of the various phases of creation – setting the earth on its foundations by splitting the primeval waters and setting the heavens in their appointed place and watering the earth with dew from its clouds – think what his revealed wisdom will do in the lives of those who find it."[6]

---

[4] Another verse in Proverbs that confirms the immeasurable wealth of wisdom is 16:16: *How much better to get wisdom than gold, to choose understanding rather than silver.*

[5] Waltke, Bruce K. *The Book of Proverbs: Chapters 1–15.* New International Commentary on the Old Testament Series. (Grand Rapids, Mich. and Cambridge, UK: William B. Eerdmans Publishing Co. 2004), 260.

[6] Ibid., 261.

Submitting to God's wisdom brings us in harmony with our Creator and because we are reconnected with Him, we can learn to live in harmony with our fellow human beings, by avoiding taking advantage of them and by refraining from abusing, harming, or falsely accusing them.

Who does not want to pursue this kind of wisdom and the blessings that result from that and that enables us to live in harmony with our fellow human beings, knowing that they cannot harm us beyond the arms of the All-Powerful and All-Wise God?

Those that have experienced this value of wisdom encourage us to acquire wisdom

> Eat honey, my son, for it is good, honey from the comb is sweat to your taste. Know also that wisdom is sweet to your soul; if you find it, there is a future hope for you, and your hope will not be cut off. (24:13,14)

The second reason the book of Proverbs gives us to embark on our quest for wisdom is through the words of those who have experienced the value of wisdom, for example, parents and teachers. Good parents and teachers encourage their children or pupils to make the pursuit of wisdom one of their main goals. They point out that nothing is more important to acquire in life than wisdom. The price for wisdom is all that you have. But it is worth it.

In the book of Proverbs, we are encouraged to pursue wisdom because it provides present health and vitality to our soul and life eternal.[7] The same blessings are mentioned in connection to fear of the Lord, linking wisdom with fear of the Lord.[8]

Wisdom is compared with honey; it has medicinal value with a sweet taste; invigorating while giving pleasure. "Wisdom has all the immediate sweetness of honey, but also the additional characteristic of a pleasure that lasts for eternity."[9]

> "Listen, my sons … Get wisdom, get understanding, do not forget my words or swerve from them. Do not forsake wisdom and she will pro-

---

[7] Proverbs 24:13,14.

[8] Proverbs 23:18.

[9] Waltke, Bruce K. *The Book of Proverbs: Chapters 15–31*. New International Commentary on the Old Testament Series. (Grand Rapids, Mich. and Cambridge, UK: William B. Eerdmans Publishing Co. 2005), 280.

tect you; love her, and she will watch over you. Wisdom is supreme, therefore get wisdom. Though it cost all you have, get understanding. Esteem her, and she will exalt you; embrace her, and she will honor you. She will set a garland of grace on your head and present you with a crown of splendor." (4:1,5–9)

This is a strong encouragement from a father or teacher to his children or pupils: Wisdom is supreme, therefore get it. "What it takes is not brains, or opportunity, but decision. Do you want it? Come and get it."[10] No price can be too high to get wisdom. Wisdom is worth all their time, energy, and resources. The dowry is nothing less than his heart.

Our pursuit of wisdom gives us several benefits, such as:

Protection. Wisdom protects us from our own wrong decisions that harm us, and wisdom protects us against others because we sense the harm, they might bring to us and therefore we keep away from them, do not associate with them nor seek their company. Wisdom protects against the evil men and women, catastrophe[11] and temptations (sexual and otherwise).

> "My son ... Say to wisdom, "You are my sister" and call understanding your kinsman; they will keep you from the adulteress, from the wayward wife with her seductive words." (7:1,4,5)

Honor. Wisdom not only protects us but also provides us with honor, respect, and reputation in the community because wisdom shapes our character. In many societies being an honorable person is of utmost value, of more importance than strength and wealth.

Wisdom herself invites us to come to her

In the book of Proverbs wisdom is not only advertised as the most valuable item to search for. Not only are we encouraged on our pursuit for wisdom by those who have experienced their richness and benefits (such as parents, teachers, and friends). In this book, wisdom is not just an abstract value, a thing, but Wisdom comes alive. It is presented to us as a person, a woman, who speaks, who invites, who challenges and who warns. This makes the pursuit of wisdom also a response to an invitation. We find that Wisdom self,

---

[10]   Kidner, *Proverbs.* 64.

[11]   Proverbs 2:12–15, 2:16–19; 5:1–20; 7, 5:22–23.

here presented to us in the metaphor of a woman, is inviting us to come to her, to pay attention to what she has to say.

> Out in the open wisdom calls aloud, she raises her voice in the public square; on top of the wall (at noisy street corners) she cries out, at the city gate she makes her speech: "How long will you who are simple love your simple ways? How long will mockers delight in mockery and fools hate knowledge? Repent at my rebuke! Then I will pour out my thoughts to you, I will make known to you, my teachings. But since you refuse to listen when I call and no one pays attention when I stretch out my hand, since you disregard all my advice and do not accept my rebuke, I in turn will laugh when disaster strikes you; I will mock when calamity overtakes you — when calamity overtakes you like a storm, when disaster sweeps over you like a whirlwind, when distress and trouble overwhelm you. Then they will call to me, but I will not answer; they will look for me but will not find me, since they hated knowledge and did not choose to fear the LORD. Since they would not accept my advice and spurned my rebuke, they will eat the fruit of their ways and be filled with the fruit of their schemes. For the waywardness of the simple will kill them, and the complacency of fools will destroy them; but whoever listens to me will live in safety and be at ease, without fear of harm." (Proverbs 1:20–33)

In this passage we learn that wisdom is **available**; one can meet her on the street corners, on our way to work, to home, while shopping, doing our business or having leisure time. Wisdom is available to each and everyone who wants it. Nevertheless, not everyone pays **attention** to her. We have a choice. We are invited, not kidnapped. We are perfectly free to not pay any attention to wisdom and to not make the quest for wisdom our highest goal. We may prefer other priorities, other ways of living. We are free to refuse to listen to what wisdom has to say and to not accept what she has to offer. But as these words make abundantly clear: there are consequences for not paying attention and these are spelled out for us. We will eat the fruit of our own choices. We will reap what we have sown. Therefore, we are warned to choose carefully. Wisdom points out that not choosing her is a foolish decision and therefore calls everyone to repent, i.e., to change their ways and to turn to wisdom. But again: although the appeal is strong and even emotional, everyone is free to disregard it. It is important, however, that we understand that wisdom is not available forever. Her offer of help and protection and life go on for a while (how long? vs 22), but it is not open-ended; her outstretched arms can be ignored and refused for a long time, but there is an expiration date for her offer.

There may come a time that we will desperately want what she has to offer (in fact, this passage seems to imply that such a time will come), but that her offer will no longer be available. This gives this passage a keen sense of urgency. We need to pay attention before it is too late. To those who do, wisdom promises true security.

> Does not wisdom call out? Does not understanding raise her voice? ² At the highest point along the way, where the paths meet, she takes her stand; beside the gate leading into the city, at the entrance, she cries aloud: "To you, O people, I call out; I raise my voice to all mankind. You who are simple, gain prudence; you who are foolish, set your hearts on it. Listen, for I have trustworthy things to say; I open my lips to speak what is right. My mouth speaks what is true, for my lips detest wickedness. All the words of my mouth are just; none of them is crooked or perverse. To the discerning all of them are right; they are upright to those who have found knowledge. Choose my instruction instead of silver, knowledge rather than choice gold, for wisdom is more precious than rubies, and nothing you desire can compare with her. I, wisdom, dwell together with prudence; I possess knowledge and discretion. To fear the LORD is to hate evil; I hate pride and arrogance, evil behavior and perverse speech. Counsel and sound judgment are mine; I have insight, I have power. By me kings reign and rulers issue decrees that are just; by me princes govern, and nobles — all who rule on earth. I love those who love me, and those who seek me find me. With me are riches and honor, enduring wealth and prosperity. My fruit is better than fine gold; what I yield surpasses choice silver. I walk in the way of righteousness, along the paths of justice, bestowing a rich inheritance on those who love me and making their treasuries full. The LORD brought me forth as the first of his works, before his deeds of old; I was formed long ages ago, at the very beginning, when the world came to be. When there were no watery depths, I was given birth, when there were no springs overflowing with water; before the mountains were settled in place, before the hills, I was given birth, before he made the world or its fields or any of the dust of the earth. I was there when he set the heavens in place, when he marked out the horizon on the face of the deep, when he established the clouds above and fixed securely the fountains of the deep, when he gave the sea its boundary so the waters would not overstep his command, and when he marked out the foundations of the earth. Then I was constantly at his side. I was filled with delight day after day, rejoicing always in his presence, rejoicing in his whole

> world and delighting in mankind. Now then, my children, listen to me; blessed are those who keep my ways. Listen to my instruction and be wise; do not disregard it. Blessed are those who listen to me, watching daily at my doors, waiting at my doorway. For those who find me find life and receive favor from the LORD. But those who fail to find me harm themselves; all who hate me love death." (Proverbs 8:1–36)

This is another powerful invitation from Wisdom, who is again described as a Woman. Again, she stands at strategic places to invite all humankind to receive what she has to offer and to choose her instead of wealth and riches. Others have recommended her to us, but now it her turn to exhibit her attractions. Wisdom is **attractive**.

She points out that those that have chosen her have not regretted it because she is morally excellent. She appeals to those that are still wondering whether to make the quest of wisdom their main objective in life. She tells them what she has to offer: insight, power, riches, honor, wealth, prosperity, even life and favor from the Lord. What more would you want? To those who wonder whether she can deliver all the goods she offers, or whether it is just empty talk, (even though she has already declared that she detests wickedness and that what she says is true), she lists her credentials. She provides us with part of her autobiography. She particularly zooms in on her relationship with the Creator. The Creator Himself considered wisdom of prime importance and used wisdom to create all there is. God used wisdom to bring order and joy into the created world. With this impressive CV she shouts again: Now then … listen to me (8: 33, 34), because if one wants to know how the world works and how to navigate life as best as possible, then we need wisdom. To those who wonder whether their quest for wisdom will be in vain, she promises that all who seek her will find her.

> Wisdom has built her house; she has set up its seven pillars. She has prepared her meat and mixed her wine; she has also set her table. She has sent out her servants, and she calls from the highest point of the city, "Let all who are simple come to my house! To those who have no sense she says, "Come, eat my food and drink the wine I have mixed. Leave your simple ways and you will live; walk in the way of insight." Whoever corrects a mocker invites insults; whoever rebukes the wicked incurs abuse. Do not rebuke mockers or they will hate you; rebuke the wise and they will love you. Instruct the wise and they will be wiser still; teach the righteous and they will add to their learning. The fear of the LORD is the beginning of wisdom, and knowledge of the Holy One is un-

derstanding. For through wisdom your days will be many, and years will be added to your life. If you are wise, your wisdom will reward you; if you are a mocker, you alone will suffer." (Proverbs 9:1–12)

This is the third time we receive an invitation from wisdom itself. Now the invitation is to have a fellowship meal with her. She has prepared a lavish banquet and issues an open invitation to all. Wisdom provides **abundance** and enjoyment. What she has to offer is marvelous. Although the invitation is open and free, it becomes clear that we will have to change directions to benefit from it. There is a need for repentance to enjoy the richness of wisdom. Not everyone is willing to do so. There are people who hear the invitation but ignore it or want to have wisdom on their own terms (without the fear of the Lord, which brings us back to the Fall in Paradise). These people will suffer the consequences of their decision.

We have seen that the quest for wisdom is very much encouraged. Wisdom is presented to us as something of the highest value that can provide us with everything we want. It is offered for free, but it is not cheap. To benefit from all its riches, we need to give up all we have. The decision is ours. Also, we must come with a right **attitude.** Wisdom is to be sought but cannot be bought; it is not mastered, but it is to be served. The book of Proverbs acknowledges that one's quest for wisdom can be with wrong motives:

> Why should a fool have money in his hand to buy wisdom, when he has no sense? (17:16)

> The mocker seeks wisdom, and finds none, but knowledge comes easily to the discerning. (14:6)

> A fool seems to think that wisdom is something you can buy, but wisdom is not something we have, but somebody we are. When one considers wisdom as a commodity, he has not understood. "Wisdom is not a commodity the proud can seize; only the humble find it."[12]

We need to create space for wisdom, not in our house, or in our barn, but in our heart, where it can become part of us. It takes humility to accept that we need wisdom. Wisdom is not our servant that we can control to accomplish our plans, but it is to be our Master, our Teacher, because she represents God's order of things and His authority.

---

[12]　Waltke, *The Book of Proverbs: Chapters 1–15*, 587.

Questions for further reflection

1. What is your ambition in life? In what way does wisdom play a role in this ambition?

2. How important on a scale of one to ten is wisdom for you? In what areas in life do you particularly need wisdom?

3. Who are the wisest people that you know and what makes them wise?

CHAPTER 2
WHAT IS WISDOM?

Wisdom is an ability to navigate life ...[13]

Having started on our quest for wisdom it is important that we have some idea what we are looking for, so that we recognize it when we see it and do not overlook it when it stares us in the face.

The question 'what is wisdom?' has been answered and is being answered in a variety of ways. There are many terms of the languages of the past that are often translated 'wisdom', such as *sophia* (Greek), *sapientia* (Latin) *hokhmah* (Hebrew), *hikma* (Arabic), *nebequ* (Akkadian) and *seboyet* (Egyptian), but it is not always clear whether these words describe wisdom in the same way.

Wisdom is a term that has transformed its specific meaning across different historical times and contexts. Although the specific meaning of wisdom has changed, it was always seen as *an ideal that involved both highest knowledge and virtuous behavior.*

Wisdom in the ancient world

Long before wisdom was analyzed in a scholarly way, wisdom was collected in 'wisdom literature.' The book of Proverbs was by no means the only book of ancient times, nor in fact the first one.

> Already in the second and third millennium B.C., wisdom literature existed ... In Mesopotamia and Egypt, for instance, government-affiliated scribe schools produced, preserved, and passed on information about the nature of the world and instructions for everyday behavior, including statements about the ability to listen, to obey, and to remain silent and maintain confidentiality. These earliest bodies of the historical wisdom literature from the third and second millennium B.C. were primarily secular. They were produced by human beings for human beings, and they were based on the belief that conduct in accordance with the stated principles results in well-being. For the most part, the content was

---

[13] Tremper Longman III, *How to Read Proverbs.* (Downers Grove: InterVarsity Press, 2002), 14–16.

conservative in approach and aimed at maintaining the power and procedures of institutions-in-charge, such as the monarchy. Only later did the role of religion in defining a body of good human conduct and finding meaning in life become more prominent.[14]

The first wisdom texts known to us are the Mesopotamian *Teachings of Shuruppak*, a collection of proverb-like sayings, dated to around 2.500 B.C. Of a somewhat later date are the Babylonian *Councils of Wisdom*.

These and other collections were used in schools as textbooks and represented the beginnings of a canon of what and how of "good" and "effective" behavior. These collections included matters such as: avoidance of bad companions, improper speech, avoidance of altercations and pacification of enemies, kindness to those in need, the duties, and benefits of religion, and behavior related to friends.

In Egypt, wisdom type writings first appeared around 2.200 B.C. with the *Precepts of Ptah-Hotep* as the oldest surviving Egyptian wisdom text. Like the earlier Mesopotamian texts, Egyptian wisdom literature (e.g., *the Instruction of Amenemope*), consisted primarily of a collection of statements about values and ways to be a productive and well-functioning member of society.

Baltes believes that the similarities in these ancient writings about the nature of wisdom are found more in the general goals, than in the specifics of content.

> These texts always record a quest for a high level of functioning of mind and personality. They are also aimed at combining the good for oneself with the good of others. Beyond such general goals, however, they vary substantially in describing what wisdom is, who possesses it, and how it can be achieved ...[15].

Baltes comments that these ancient wisdom writings have made several contributions to our understanding of wisdom, namely: wisdom is broad and multi-faceted; wisdom is an extraordinary and superior attribute; wisdom deals with the known, the uncertain, and the not known; the acquisition of wisdom requires mentorship and is a life-long task; there is an intimate connection be-

---

[14] Baltes, Paul B. *Wisdom as Orchestration of Mind and Virtue*. Max Planck Institute for Human Development, Berlin Book in preparation, 2004 https://library.mpib-berlin.mpg.de/ft/pb/PB_Wisdom_2004.pdf, 44.

[15] Baltes, 70, 71.

tween intellect (knowledge) and virtue (character/personality); there is a close relationship between religion and wisdom.[16]

Wisdom from the East

China made significant early contributions to the wisdom literature. Confucius (551–479 B.C.) is considered even today by many Chinese as the "Supreme Sage."

> … the Confucian writings describe wisdom as an integrated and highly developed state of mind and character. A corpus of specific proverbs, maxims, and aphorisms is also part of the teachings. The teachings, however, include an organized description of the entire frame of the cultivated "wise" or sage person. Wisdom, or the sage, is defined primarily by an ideal person, the "most complete" …, or the "superior" man (chün-tzu) … Thus, for Confucius, wisdom was definitely an integrated whole of perfection: in mind, personality, and social productivity.[17]

Confucian wisdom is collected in the *Analects of Confucius*, a document that still has profound influence on Chinese culture and East Asia.

Gautama Buddha (563 B.C.–483 B.C.), the founder of **Buddhism** also spoke and wrote about wisdom, which in his understanding was a state of personal Enlightenment.

> … the phrase "the Wisdom of Buddhism" denotes a large body of writings that stretches across a wide field, including the wisdom of the principal followers of the original Gautama Buddha and that of the leading minds among his many followers. Buddhist wisdom is an evolving process. Through the centuries it has been achieved and created by the spiritual experiences of each generation of Buddhas and their practices as they attempt to achieve Enlightenment.[18]

In Buddhism, "wisdom" ('pranja' or 'panna') is realizing or perceiving the true nature of reality; seeing things as they are, not as they appear. This wisdom is not bound by conceptual knowledge. It must be intimately experienced to be understood."[19]

---

[16]   Baltes, 69–75.

[17]   Baltes, 50.

[18]   Baltes, 52, 53.

[19]   https://www.thoughtco.com/prajna-or-panna-449852.

Wisdom in the Greek philosophers: Socrates, Plato, and Aristotle

The first philosophical analysis of wisdom started with the Greek philosophers, like Socrates, Plato, and Aristotle, who are the founders of Western philosophy.

Each of them made wisdom a topic of philosophical analysis. When philosophy (= love of wisdom) emerged as a field of study, wisdom was part of the agenda.

Baltes believes that Socrates (470–399 B.C.) made three specific contributions to a philosophy of wisdom

> First, he successfully shifted the central problem of philosophy from cosmology to the formulation of rules of life and the nature of the soul. His second contribution was the use of "Socratic" dialogues to define and question ways to think and ways to behave … In the context of his discourses, Socrates … advanced a feature of wisdom that has become an essential part of the definition of wisdom in the Western world. He argued that, if there is one respect in which he was wiser than others, it is that he understood his own ignorance – that he knew that he didn't know. Socrates … third contribution to the philosophy of wisdom … deals with his way of understanding the intimate connection between mind and virtue … "all virtue is knowledge" and "human wisdom (is) the expert knowledge of virtue."[20]

For Plato (428–347 B.C.), wisdom was

> "An intellectual and contemplative virtue, a knowledge of eternal, immutable, and intelligible Ideas. Platonic wisdom … is knowledge of the ideal and therefore divine. God is wise; man is a lover of wisdom who tries to become wise … Plato … did not … propose that wisdom is a human product. Rather, his theory of Form and Ideas located wisdom in a metaphysical sphere whose foundation is in the divine; it can only be approximated by humans. For Plato … only God is wise; man can only be a friend of wisdom, a seeker of wisdom."[21]

Aristotle (384–322 B.C.) viewed wisdom as largely the product of human development.

> "According to Aristotle, humans through a combination of speculative and empirical efforts, through experience-guided individual develop-

---

[20] Baltes, 84.

[21] Baltes, 85, 86.

> ment, can produce and attain wisdom. Reaching the perfect, "ideal" state of wisdom may not be possible, but this is for human reasons and not because the source of wisdom is inherently divine. Divine and metaphysical things are part of the domain of knowledge associated with wisdom but being divine is not necessary for acquiring wisdom. The second important part of Aristotle's treatment of wisdom is the intimate connection between morality, ethics, and wisdom-related knowledge that is part of his conception of eudaimonia … To be wise is to strive for a condition of eudaimonia or what we now might call moral perfection. … For Aristotle, … the mark of wisdom is the very character of the person. Part of an excellent character is having virtues … such as a sense of justice and courage and achieving temperance in the regulation of one's emotions. … Aristotle distinguished between theoretical wisdom (theoria or sophia) and practical wisdom (phronesis). Theoretical wisdom is contemplative and devoted to the search for knowledge and truth for their own sake. It also includes "abstract" knowledge about the order and causes of things. Practical wisdom deals with knowledge translated into action, producing outcomes. The phronimos, the practically wise person, is able to judge correctly about the ends of action as well as the proper means to attain them."[22]

Baltes derived the following conclusions of his treatment of wisdom in ancient Greek philosophy.

> First, … wisdom is a matter of utmost excellence (or even absolute truth) in knowledge; it deals with the conduct and interpretation of life; it involves an intimate connection between mind and character; it deals with theoretical knowledge and practical application; and it represents an ideal that can be approximated only. Second … the Greek trio of philosophers took an explicit step toward an analytical and secular treatment of wisdom. Beginning with Socrates and reaching a first culmination in Aristotle, wisdom became a matter of science and not only religious tradition.[23]

Wisdom in the Early Middle Ages

Judeo-Christian philosophy transported the idea of wisdom from antiquity into the Middle Ages. For Augustine (396–430), an Algerian-Roman theologian and

---

[22] Baltes, 88–90.

[23] Baltes, 91.

one of the most influential philosophers in Western Christianity, wisdom was an important theme in his writings and his understanding of wisdom dominated the Middle Ages for a long time.

> He limited wisdom to knowledge of divine things and allocated knowledge of human things to scientia. For Augustine the seeking of wisdom was founded in the worship of the Christian God.[24]

While hitherto the terms *sapientia* (wisdom) and *scientia* (science, knowledge) had been held together, Augustine separated them, proposing "that intellectual knowledge of eternal things pertains to wisdom, and rational knowledge of temporal things to science."[25]

For Augustine wisdom is assigned to the superior part of reason and science is assigned to the lower part.[26] He stated that the superior part of reason is focused on supernal reasons for the sake of both contemplation and practical counsel.[27] Both are needed, but in the right order. Scientia (knowledge), while subordinated to wisdom, has a prominent place: it aids both in acquiring and in applying wisdom.[28]

Islamic wisdom

From the ninth century onwards Arab (Muslim) scholars also began addressing the topic of wisdom. *Al Kindi* (801–873), one of the first Islamic philosophers, justified his search for wisdom with the following words:

> After all, Muhammed had said, 'Wisdom is the believer's straying camel; he takes it from wherever he may find it and does not care from which vessel it has issued.'[29]

---

[24] Baltes, 92, 93.

[25] Trowbridge, Richard Hawley. "The Scientific Approach of Wisdom", doctoral dissertation (2005 Union Institute & University Cincinnati, Ohio), page 33; http://www.wisdompage.com/TheScientificApproachtoWisdom.doc.

[26] Kowalczyk, Stanislaw, "Topicality of St. Augustine's Concept of Wisdom" *Dialogue and Universalism*, Volume 16, Issue 5/6, 2006, pages 83–89; https://doi.org/10.5840/du2006165/667.

[27] Quoted in Leonard Swidler "A Christian Historical Perspective on Wisdom" *Journal of Ecumenical Studies*, 33:4, Fall 1996.

[28] Trowbridge, 33.

[29] Le Gai Eaton, Charles. *Islam and the Destiny of Man* (Albany: SUNY, 1986), 35.

Al Farabi (870–950), who is described as one of the most original thinkers among the Arabs, sought to establish the relationship between wisdom and Greek philosophy with Islamic sharia.[30]

Ibn Sina (980–1037) argued that wisdom helps humans attain perfection. He believed that reason, knowledge, and truth are the pathways to true wisdom.[31]

Al Ghazali (1058–1111), who is sometimes referred to as the greatest Muslim after Muhammad, defined wisdom as 'knowledge of the most excellent things through the use of science', however he added that the best knowledge is the knowledge of God, as God is the most excellent most wise.[32]

Wisdom in the late Middle Ages

Thomas Aquinas (1224–1274), an Italian theologian and a very influential Christian philosopher, also had a great deal to say about wisdom. He did not separate wisdom and science, but as Aristotle had done, he separated *prudentia* (prudence, phronesis) from *sapientia* (wisdom):

> It is evident that prudence is wisdom in human affairs, it is not, however, simply wisdom, as it is not simply concerned with the highest cause, being concerned with the good for humans; and Homo is not the best of those things that are. And for that reason, it is expressly stated that prudence is wisdom for a man, not however wisdom simply.[33]

While, according to Aquinas, wisdom is a theological virtue, prudence is one of the most important cardinal virtues. "Thus, prudentia indeed holds an exceptionally high place for Aquinas, even if lacking the sublimity of sapientia."[34]

Aquinas considered wisdom as one of the seven gifts of the Holy Spirit (along with understanding, counsel/right judgment, courage, knowledge, piety, fear of God).

---

[30] Abdul Hakim Abdullah & Kabara Auwal Halabi "The Wisdom: A Concept of Character Building Based on Islamic View." *International Journal of Academic Research in Business and Social Sciences* 2017, Vol. 7, No. 5.

[31] Ibid.

[32] Field, Claud, *Wisdom of the East, the Confessions of Al Ghazzali: Translated for the First Time into English.* (London: Forgotten Books, 2008).

[33] Trowbridge, 35.

[34] Ibid, 35.

> It belongs to the wisdom that is an intellectual virtue to pronounce right judgment about Divine things after reason has made its inquiry, but it belongs to wisdom as a gift of the Holy Ghost to judge aright about them on account of connaturality with them (Summa IIª-IIae Q45A2co).[35]

Baltes believes that the overall thinking on wisdom in the Middle Ages is that wisdom is the capstone of human excellence.

> Wisdom continued to be seen as excellence in mind and character, as a concern for the conduct and meaning of life, as something that is guided foremost by criteria of individual well-being and the good of humankind, and finally, as something where at least parts of it can be acquired and practiced.[36]

Renaissance and Enlightenment: the secularization of wisdom

After the Middle Ages, during the Renaissance (14th–16th century) and continuing in the Enlightenment (16th–18th century), what was already dormant became more visible: the secularization of wisdom.

> Perhaps the secularization of wisdom has been the primary factor in the "modern" crisis of wisdom and related concepts such as progress … or … the modern "decline" of wisdom.[37]

Wisdom became a human perfection, a human goal, a human accomplishment. One of the main influencers in this process was the French philosopher and theologian *Pierre Charron* (1541–1603).

> Charron, … by his profound split of faith and reason, by his decision to exclude matters of the divine from the domain of wisdom, and by his allocation of the primary source of wisdom to "natural" human conditions (although preconditioned by God), represents one prototype of the Renaissance secularization of the idea of wisdom. Wisdom became an autonomous and naturally acquired moral virtue and not a divine property that we can obtain only through the practice of religion, revelation, and grace.[38]

---

[35] Ibid, 39, 40.

[36] Baltes, 96.

[37] Baltes, 98.

[38] Baltes, 101.

As the divine was moved to the background, wisdom seemed to have lost its power as an organizing and explanatory system. During the Enlightenment of the 18th century divine and traditional conceptions of authority were critically reexamined and new forms of human reason and social arrangements were explored.

The consequences of this for the concept and importance of wisdom, can particularly be seen by *Immanuel Kant* (1724–1804).

> Wisdom, … for Kant, in line with the emphasis of the Enlightenment on reason …, is a human product for humans. It is not speculation or revelation. Whatever wisdom involves, it needs to be in concert with our scientific knowledge about the nature of the world. With this general approach to wisdom, Kant exemplifies the philosophical accomplishments of the Enlightenment: the increasing focus on philosophy as the activity of humans for humans. At the same time that he argues that reason (the intellect) in itself is constrained and has limits, Kant challenges what humans alone can accomplish. Reason "precipitates itself into darkness and contradictions" unless we know what we cannot know and why we cannot know it. Even within these limitations, however, human wisdom for Kant is "the idea of the rule-perfected practical use of reason" … Kant also makes clear that wisdom is different from other concepts such as prudence or sagacity … in that these, contrary to wisdom, are not always guided by consideration of morality and the wellbeing of others. Kant … perhaps more than anybody else during the Enlightenment, made clear that wisdom, representing a utopian vision, is more than a human … can achieve. Kant suggests that wisdom, despite his valiant efforts to bring much of it under human control, is ultimately beyond reach."[39]

Wisdom in modern times

During the Renaissance and the Enlightenment philosophy became separated from theology and with the rejection of figures of authority, including God and His revelation as seen in Scripture, wisdom was viewed *"not as philosophically or empirically grounded truth, but as a high level of knowledge about the human condition that is based on multiple forms and bodies of evidence."*[40]

---

[39]   Baltes, 110–112.

[40]   Baltes, 113.

Gradually, we see another concept of wisdom develop namely as a "high level of common-sense knowledge about life."[41]

The German philosopher *Arthur Schopenhauer* (1788–1860), defined wisdom as follows:

> It seems to me that wisdom is not only theoretical but also practical perfection. I would define wisdom as the complete and true knowledge of things in the whole and general, a state of knowledge that has permeated … the individual human … so totally manifested in his actions as a regulatory force and for all his behavior.[42]

The secularization of wisdom continues in our modern times. Among (western) philosophers it is now widely accepted that wisdom is not primarily divine and based on revelation.

> … it would be difficult to imagine that any modern philosophical conception of wisdom would not be based primarily on the results of human activity and human insights.[43]

Of course, among theologians and scholars in the tradition of religious studies, the spiritual dimension of wisdom is dominant.

Baltes concludes:

> This review of twentieth-century commentary points to the conclusion that philosophers have completed the journey that started millennia ago when wisdom was taken from heaven to earth, during the Renaissance and the Enlightenment, when the foundation of wisdom was located in the mind of human beings and their recognition of the evidence. Modern philosophers have added to this human aspect reasons for the conclusion that wisdom as an ideal body of knowledge and judgment about the conduct and meaning of life is not possible.[44]

Analyzing 20th century philosophical writings, Baltes lists the following characteristics of wisdom:[45]

- Wisdom is life-orientation and action-guiding knowledge dealing with a good life.

---

[41] Baltes, 118.

[42] Baltes, 115, 116.

[43] Baltes, 131.

[44] Baltes, 131, 132.

[45] Baltes, 132, 133.

- Wisdom is holistic, integrative, and balanced knowledge.
- Wisdom is knowledge about limits and uncertainty.
- Wisdom is knowledge about pluralism and tolerance of diversity.
- Wisdom implies a principle of sensitivity toward other forms of thinking and other ways of living, a farewell to any notion of the absolute in questions of optimality.
- Wisdom is experiential knowledge.
- Wisdom is justified knowledge and needs to consider multiple sources of knowledge as part of its foundation.

Defining wisdom

Even though the quest for wisdom is as old as mankind, there is no consensus among philosophers (who are, after all, lovers *phileō* of wisdom *sophía*) and religious people, who for centuries monopolized the domain of wisdom, about how to define wisdom. During the last two decades, researchers in the behavioral sciences also have shown renewed interest in the concept of wisdom, which has historically been considered the pinnacle of human development. However, an agreed-upon definition of wisdom does not yet exist.

To define wisdom, we can differentiate between *implicit* theoretical approaches to wisdom and *explicit* theoretical approaches to wisdom. Implicit theoretical approaches search for an understanding of people's folk conceptions of what wisdom is. Explicit theories are constructions of expert theorists and researchers rather than laypeople. Most explicit-theoretical approaches to wisdom are based on constructs from the psychology of human development.

Three major contemporary explicit-theoretical models of wisdom proposed by psychologists shed light on what the world has to offer by way of defining wisdom.

Baltes: Wisdom as Expert Knowledge about the fundamental pragmatics of human life[46]

Paul B. Baltes (1939–2006) was one of the first and most important scientists in empirical wisdom research. For twenty years, he, along with several col-

---

[46] Baltes P.B. & Smith, J. (1990b). "Towards a psychology of wisdom and its ontogenesis." In R.J. Sternberg (Ed.), *Wisdom – Its nature, origins, and development*, 87–120) (Cambridge, UK: Cambridge University Press, 1990); Also: Baltes, P.B. & Staudinger, U. (2000). "Wisdom: A metaheuristic (pragmatic) to orchestrate mind and virtue toward excellence." *American Psychologist*, 55(1), 122–136.

leagues of the Max Planck Institute for Human Development in Berlin, conducted a research program on the psychology of wisdom.

In the Berlin wisdom paradigm, wisdom is defined as *"Expert knowledge about the fundamental pragmatics of human life."* With 'fundamental pragmatics', they mean knowledge and judgment about the essence of the human condition and the ways and means of planning, managing, and understanding a good life.[47]

Baltes and his colleagues of the Berlin group made clear that their emphasis is on wisdom as a body of knowledge and not on wise individuals.

> Our conception of wisdom entails more than the mind and personality of individuals. In our conception, wisdom is fundamentally a cultural and collective product in which individuals participate. Individuals are only some of the carriers and outcomes of wisdom.[48]

They believe that wise persons represent but one carrier of wisdom-related knowledge. Other carriers of wisdom-related knowledge they mention are texts of social institutions (e.g., a constitution or the law of a country), religious documents, collections of proverbs and prescriptions about values and human conduct.

---

[47] For Baltes the five criteria of wisdom-related knowledge are:
  (a) rich factual knowledge about life (general and specific knowledge about the conditions of life and its variations).
  (b) rich procedural knowledge about life (general and specific knowledge about strategies of judgment and advice concerning matters of life).
  (c) life span contextualism (knowledge about the contexts of life and their temporal (developmental) relationships).
  (d) relativism of values and life priorities (knowledge about differences in values, goals, and priorities).
  (e) recognition and management of uncertainty (knowledge about the relative indeterminacy and unpredictability of life and ways to manage).

  These five criteria of wisdom are presented as 'ideals', as a set of characteristics that should be evident in a given body of knowledge about the fundamental pragmatics of life to approximate wisdom as Baltes has defined it.

[48] Baltes, P.B., & Staudinger, U.M. (2000). "Wisdom: A metaheuristic (pragmatic) to orchestrate mind and virtue toward excellence." *American Psychologist*, 55(1), 122–136.

Sternberg: A Balance Theory of Wisdom[49]

Robert J. Sternberg (1949–), President of the American Psychological Association, and one of the major researchers on wisdom, defines wisdom as the use of one's intelligence, creativity, common sense, and knowledge and as mediated by positive ethical values toward the achievement of a common good through a balance among (a) intrapersonal (one's own), (b) interpersonal (others), and (c) extrapersonal (institutional and other larger) interests, over the (a) short and (b) long terms to achieve a balance among (a) adaptation to existing environments, (b) shaping of existing environments, and (c) selection of new environments.[50]

Wisdom is practical intelligence applied to a balance of intrapersonal, interpersonal, and extrapersonal interests. It is a special case of practical intelligence, one that requires balancing of multiple and often competing interests.

Ardelt: wisdom as cognitive, reflective, and affective integration[51]

Monika Ardelt, Associate Professor of Sociology at The University of Florida, and one of the leading wisdom theorists and researchers, developed the *Three-Dimensional Wisdom Theory* In this she defines wisdom as an integration of cognitive, reflective, and affective dimensions.

The *cognitive dimension of wisdom* refers to a person's ability to understand life, that is, to comprehend the significance and deeper meaning of phenomena and events, particularly regarding intrapersonal and interpersonal matters. This includes knowledge of the positive and negative aspects of human nature, of the inherent limits of knowledge, and of life's unpredictability and uncertainties.

---

[49] Sternberg, Robert J. "A Balance Theory of Wisdom." *Review of General Psychology*, 1998, 2(4), 347–365.

[50] http://www.robertjsternberg.com/wisdom. The view of wisdom proposed by Sternberg has at the core the notion of tacit knowledge about oneself, others, and situational contexts. Sternberg's understanding of tacit knowledge is that it is action oriented, typically acquired without direct help from others, and allows individuals to achieve goals they personally value. Tacit knowledge has three main features: (a) it is procedural; (b) it is relevant to the attainment of goals people value; and (c) it typically is acquired with little help from others. Tacit knowledge is an important part of practical intelligence.

[51] Ardelt, Monica. "Empirical Assessment of a Three-Dimensional Wisdom Scale" *Research on Aging*, Vol. 25 No. 3, May 2003 275–324.

The *reflective dimension* refers to reflective thinking by looking at phenomena and events from many different perspectives to develop self-awareness and self-insight.

The *affective dimension* of wisdom refers to the presence of positive emotions and behavior toward other beings, such as feelings and acts of sympathy and compassion, and the absence of indifferent or negative emotions and behavior toward others.

The three dimensions must be simultaneously present for a person to be considered "wise". That means that according to Ardelt, a person would be wise, if (a) he/she understands life and has a desire to know the truth, (b) perceives phenomena from multiple perspectives and, (c) loves others sympathetically and compassionately.

She admits that only very few people might exist that would satisfy this definition of a wise person. Although wisdom per se might be difficult to find, it should still be possible to assess how close people come to this ideal state.[52]

Wisdom as defined by the world

We should not be surprised that in our modern times, when wisdom has been secularized, that most researchers tend to define wisdom in secular terms, not spiritual.

Based on his analysis and synthesis of cultural-historical and philosophical work Baltes identified seven properties of wisdom that are, if not universally, accepted as inherent in any definition of wisdom:

1. Wisdom addresses important and difficult questions and strategies about the conduct and meaning of life.

2. Wisdom includes knowledge about the limits of knowledge and the uncertainties of the world.

3. Wisdom represents a truly superior level of knowledge, judgment, and advice.

---

[52] Ardelt differentiates between wisdom and intellectual knowledge. For example, while the primary goal of intellectual knowledge according to Ardelt is a quantitative accumulation of information, the fundamental goal of wisdom is a qualitative understanding of phenomena.

4. Wisdom constitutes knowledge with extraordinary scope, depth, and balance.

5. Wisdom involves a perfect synergy of mind and character, that is, an orchestration of knowledge and virtues.

6. Wisdom represents knowledge used for the good or well-being of oneself and that of others.

7. Wisdom, though difficult to achieve and to specify, is easily recognized when manifested.[53]

One wonders whether there has ever been someone or ever will be a person who has mastered this ability to perfection. Even the contemporary experts on wisdom admit that model examples of perfect wisdom are hard to find. They admit that they have constructed an ideal type of a wise person and realize that "very few people, even among those who are generally considered wise, might measure up to this ideal type."[54]

If we cannot find a human being that demonstrates perfect wisdom all the time, we need to look elsewhere as J.I. Packer points out:

> Wisdom is the power to see, and the inclination to choose, the best and highest goal, together with the surest means of attaining it. Wisdom is, in fact, the practical side of moral goodness. As such, it is found in its fullness only in God. He alone is naturally and entirely and invariable wise.[55]

---

[53] Baltes, 17. Beyond these agreed upon universal views on wisdom, other properties could be considered. For instance, there is the question of types of wisdom. Because wisdom is so complex and multifaceted, it is argued that not all aspects of wisdom cannot be in any single person, that there is a need for specialization with different people holding the key to different aspects of wisdom. Imagine the requirements one would need to display the full range of theoretical and practical skills involved in the conduct of life or the full spectrum of relevant emotions, including melancholy and optimism. Aleida Assmann (1991), because of her historical analyses, distinguishes, for instance, between parental-authoritative wisdom, judicial or kingly wisdom, magical wisdom, and skeptical wisdom. (Baltes, 20).

[54] Ardelt, M. "Where can wisdom be found: A Reply to the Commentaries by Baltes and Kunzmann, Sternberg, and Achenbaum." Human Development 2004; 47:304–307.

[55] Packer, J.I. *Knowing God*, (London: Hodder and Stoughton, 2013), 100.

Wisdom as defined by the Bible

The most common word in the Old Testament used for wisdom is the Hebrew word *hokmah*. This word means 'masterful understanding', or 'skill', or 'expertise', or 'ability.' Although the word 'hokmah' is most often translated by 'wisdom', sometimes it is called 'skill' or 'ability'. The adjective 'hakam' is mostly translated as 'wise' but sometimes also as 'craftsman', 'skilled' or 'skillful'.[56]

Hokmah is used to describe technical and artistic skill (craftsmen who made priestly garments, female weavers; artisans who designed and constructed the tabernacle, goldsmiths); skill of making war; skill to govern or to sail, skill in leadership or in farming; skilled in lamentation; skilled magicians and soothsayers; skilled military strategists and statesman; skilled merchants and skilled woodsmen.[57]

The word *hokmah* refers to a skill of one sort or another. This can be technical expertise and other professional capabilities of several types. A wise man is someone who has mastered something. The wise person was highly practical, not merely theoretical. He or she was interested in being able to formulate the sorts of plans that would help produce the desired results in life for themselves and for the welfare of others. *Hokmah* (wisdom) is not primarily abstract, never merely a matter of knowing facts. It is knowing what to do with them, and consequently, doing it. *Hokmah* refers to the practical ability to apply theory to practice.

> Biblical wisdom to a significant extent has to do with practical knowledge, with a know-how regarding the whole spectrum of human skills and activities, all in tune with the normative patterns and possibilities – and with the concrete givens – of creation.[58]

---

[56] Sources: Young, Robert. *Young's Analytical Concordance to the Bible.* (Illinois: Tyndale House Publishers House, 1984; Strong, James. *Strong's Exhaustive Concordance of the Bible.* (Peabody, Massachusetts: Hendrickson Publishers, 2007). Wilson, William. *Wilson's Old Testament Word Studies.* (Peabody, Massachusetts: Hendrickson Publishers, 1990).

[57] References: Ex. 28:3; Ex. 35:25, 26; Ex. 31:3, 35:30–36:1; Jer. 10:9; Is. 10:13; Jer. 50:35; Ps. 107:27; Ez. 27:8; Deut. 34:9; Is. 29:14; Is. 28:23–29; Jer. 9:17; Gen. 41:8; Is. 44:25; Is. 29:14; Jer. 49:7; Ez. 28:4,5; 1 Kings 5:6.

[58] Van Leeuwen, Raymond. "Building God's House – an exploration in Wisdom" – In *The way of wisdom: Essay in Honor of Bruce K. Waltke* J.I. Packer, Sven K. Soderlund (eds) (Grand Rapids, Michigan: Zondervan Publishing House, 2000) 205, 206.

When we look at the book of Proverbs, we learn that *Hokmah* focuses on the skill for living as God intends, the ability to get along successfully with God and with men.

The book of Proverbs claims to offer *hokmah* to the reader. The words "wise" and "wisdom" occur about 125 times in Proverbs.

> Hokmah, in Proverbs, focuses on the application of moral and ethical principles to the living of life, so that one might be said to 'live skillfully', 'as compared to a sailor who might sail skillfully or a metal worker who might craft metal skillfully. A person with wisdom has expertise in living in a way that makes life go as well as possible for him.'[59]

> In Proverbs, wisdom means being skillful and successful in one's relationships and responsibilities. It involves observing and following the Creator's principles of order in the moral universe. This order manifests God's wisdom. To the extent man follows this order, he is wise.[60]

The wisdom that is presented to us in the book of Proverbs is wisdom expressed in three levels: practical, ethical, and theological.

> Our understanding of the nature of wisdom in the book of Proverbs is that it is more than practical advice for how to live in the world. Wisdom is ethical and foundationally theological. One cannot be called wise unless one has a proper relationship with Yahweh.[61]

We will look at what this means in more detail in the next chapter.

Questions for further reflection

1. How would you define wisdom?

2. Mention some of the main ethical values that influence your decisions.

3. Who do you turn to for advice when you need to make an important decision in your life?

---

[59] Anders, Max, *Proverbs*, Holman Old Testament Commentary, (Nashville, Tennessee: Broadman and Holman Publishers, 2005), 19.

[60] Zuck, Roy B. "A Theology of the Wisdom Books and the Song of Songs," in *A Biblical Theology of the Old Testament* (Zuck, ed.) (Chicago: Moody Publishers, 1991), 232.

[61] Tremper Longman III, *The Fear of the Lord is Wisdom*, (Grand Rapids, Michigan: Baker Academic, 2017), 25.

CHAPTER 3
THE FOUNDATION OF WISDOM:
THE FEAR OF THE LORD

The fear of the LORD is the beginning of wisdom,
and knowledge of the Holy One is understanding (Proverbs 9:10)

Having heard about the tremendous richness of wisdom and being encouraged by those who have gone before as well as having heard the invitation of wisdom itself, we have started on our quest for wisdom. As a first step we have defined what we are looking for, when searching for wisdom. With this came the sobering thought that no one, except God, has demonstrated to perfection what it is to possess wisdom. This could discourage us from continuing our quest, because we may never be able to get there or, when we get there, we may not be able to stay there all the time. On the other hand, knowing that only God is All Wise all the time, we might want to explore whether He might be able and willing to help us move on with our quest.

We have seen that the first humans set out on their quest for wisdom for their own advantage, to become like God. This brought them into deep trouble.

> Wisdom and egocentricity are incompatible … people who have gotten where they are by not taking other people's interests into account or even by actively thwarting the interests of others … would not be viewed as wise.[62]

In his book *Why Smart People Can be so Stupid*[63] psychologist Robert Sternberg suggests that intelligent, well-educated people are particularly susceptible to five fallacies that inhibit wise choices and actions:

- **Unrealistic optimism**, whereby one believes one is so smart or powerful that it is pointless to worry about the outcomes, and especially the

---

[62] Sternberg, Robert J. "A balance theory of wisdom." *Review of General Psychology*, Vol 2(4), Dec 1998, 347–365.

[63] Sternberg, Robert J. *Why Smart People Can be so Stupid* (New Haven: Yale University Press, 2003), See also Stenberg's article "Why smart people can be so foolish." *European Psychologist*, (2004) 9 (3), 145–150.

long-term ones, of what one does because everything will come out all right.

- **Egocentrism**, thinking that the world revolves, or at least should revolve, around them. Acting in ways that benefit themselves, regardless of how that behavior affects others.

- **Omniscience**, believing that one knows all there is to know and therefore does not have to listen to the advice and counsel of others.

- **Omnipotence**, believing that one's intelligence and education somehow make you all-powerful.

- **Invulnerability**, whereby you believe that you will get away with whatever you do, no matter how inappropriate or irresponsible it may be.

Sternberg calls this 'the imbalance theory of foolishness.' This theory views foolishness as the opposite of wisdom. In Sternberg's understanding individuals are foolish when they lack the ability to balance interests and, therefore, do not achieve a common good.

The book of Proverbs is fully aware of these fallacies and points out that wisdom sought for our own advantage will bring us into confrontation with our Creator. Mere human how-to knowledge is not enough. Wisdom is distinct from intelligence as measured by IQ tests. The foundation for our quest for wisdom cannot be our own self-interest but must be something else.

The book of Proverbs emphasizes a vital ingredient of being wise, namely ***fearing the LORD***. This fear of the LORD stands in opposition to being wise in one's own eyes and we hear: *"Do not be wise in your own eyes; fear the LORD and shun evil."* (Proverbs 3:7)

Fearing the LORD acknowledges that we are not an autonomous, independent species, but that we are under the authority of a Sovereign Creator, to whom we are accountable.

> The fear of the Lord in the book of Proverbs amounts to religion as we understand it today. By fear of the Lord these sages called attention to religious devotion in the richest sense of the phrase. It meant, purely and simply, that which every human being owes the Creator.[64]

---

[64] Crenshaw, James L. *Old Testament Wisdom; An Introduction.* (London: SCM Press Ltd, 1982), 95.

The fear of the LORD is:

> The first, foundational, and controlling principle that saturates the intellectual, moral, and practical elements of the wisdom taught in Proverbs. Apart from that perspective knowledge may delete God and become futile and destructive. The absence or presence of the fear of the Lord decides whether a proverb is acceptable or not, whether it is true or false.[65]

> The concept of 'fearing Yahweh' thus included every aspect of Israel's relationship to him: obedience, loyalty, worship, sacrifice and love.[66]

The beginning of wisdom

The term 'the fear of the LORD' can be considered the motto of the book of Proverbs. The term occurs twenty times in the book of Proverbs. The first time is in the prologue in 1:7 and the last time is in one of the last verses of the book (31:30). This underlines that the concept is foundational to the book. Several the explicit references to the fear of the LORD are frequently placed in prominent positions near the beginnings and ends of chapters, and often introduce or form climaxes to groups of verses, bringing proverbs about human conduct into close association with God's actions and overarching control of society, so that it is made clear that true wisdom comes through proper acknowledgement of Him.[67]

> What the alphabet is to reading, notes to reading music, and numerals to mathematics, the fear of the Lord is to attaining the revealed knowledge of this book.[68]

The importance of fear of God for wisdom is found in Proverbs 9:10 (and 1:7), where we read: *"The fear of the LORD is the beginning of Wisdom."* The Hebrew word used here for 'beginning' (*resit*) means 'starting point' and can be translated as 'the essence', or 'the principle' or 'the root'.

> The word 'beginning' used here refers to first and controlling principle, rather than a stage which one leaves behind."[69]

---

[65]   Woodcock, Eldon; *Proverbs, A Topical Study.* (Grand Rapids, Michigan: Zondervan, 2001), 51,52.

[66]   Whybray, R.N. *Wisdom in Proverbs* (London: SCM, 1965), 96,97.

[67]   Whybray, R.N. *The Book of Proverbs: A Survey of Modern Study.* HBIS 1. (Leiden: Brill. 1995), 139.

[68]   Waltke, 181.

Wisdom is rooted in and derives from the fear of the LORD. The fear of the LORD is the precondition for wisdom. The fear of the LORD is the essential source, the fundamental principle of wisdom. If we want to gain wisdom, we must start with developing a fear of the LORD. Without fear of the LORD, one cannot acquire true wisdom.

> Wisdom is to be found with God, and nowhere else, and unless the quest for wisdom brings a man to his knees in awe and reverence, knowing his own helplessness to make himself wise, wisdom remains for him a closed book.[70]

Those who want to be wise need first to develop a reverence toward, dependence upon, humility before, worship of, and obedience to, God. The book of Proverbs teaches us that wisdom is not simply a matter of learning certain rules and applying them mechanically, but at its core is the relationship with God. Wisdom, which as we have seen, is the skill to navigate life successfully, cannot be gained independently from the Giver of life, the Creator. God created the world through His wisdom and His creation reflects this wisdom in several ways. His wisdom maintains the order in the universe. This means that only in a close relationship with Him we will be able to learn the competence to navigate our life successfully, the skill to speak and act in a healthy way etc.

The reason this is the beginning of wisdom is that

> If you have this response to being in God's presence, then you know your rightful position in the universe. And if you don't, then you have a fundamental misunderstanding of who you are in God's world.[71]

Wisdom reflects the correct attitude to life, and this begins with a right attitude to God. When we want to learn to steer through life successfully, we must begin by acknowledging the necessity of God in our quest for wisdom.

What does 'the fear of the LORD' mean?

Fear of God, which as we have seen is the essential source and fundamental principle of wisdom, is a phrase that is not common today. Our parents or grandparents spoke of god-fearing people, but this term seems to disappear

---

[69]   Kidner, 56.

[70]   Toombs, Lawrence E. "O.T. Theology and the Wisdom Literature." *Journal of Bible and Religion* 23 (1952), 195.

[71]   Source unknown.

rapidly nowadays. When you look up the word 'god-fearing' in a dictionary you learn that it is said of someone who is 'devout', or 'deeply religious' or of a person that has 'a reverent feeling toward God', or of 'religious people who try to obey the rules of their religion and to live in a way that is considered morally right'.

The term is not a very appealing one at first sight. How many of us would want to call ourselves 'God-fearers? Even our friends might wonder: should one not **love** God instead of **fear** God? Is God Someone to be feared? Nevertheless, we read that people like Abraham, Joseph, Obadiah, Nehemiah, Hezekiah, Job and Jonah all feared God.[72] In their contexts the phrase is like "committed to" or "trusting in" God. Some have called the fear of the LORD 'the soul of godliness.'[73]

Sometimes 'the fear of the LORD' is another word for 'worshipping God'.

> The phrase 'fear of the Lord' capsulates the totality of man's religious faith. It is comprehensive term for the worship of the Lord, or religion.[74]

The fear of the LORD refers to "religious devotion in the richest sense of the phrase."[75]

In the New Testament we do not find this expression 'fear of the LORD' mentioned very often[76], but there we read about 'faith', which, according to some Bible scholars, expresses a similar truth: *"To fear the Lord is to commit oneself to Him in faith and this faith includes the believer's obedience, loyalty and love."*[77]

---

[72] References: Gen. 22:12; Gen. 42:18, 1 Kings 18:12; Nehemiah 5:15; Jeremiah 26:19; Job 1:1; Jonah 1:9.

[73] Murray, John. *Principles of Conduct* (Grand Rapids, Eerdmans, 1957), 229.

[74] Hassell Bullock, C. *An Introduction to the Old Testament Poetic Books.* (Chicago: Moody, 1988), 52.

[75] Crenshaw, James L. *Old Testament Wisdom; An Introduction.* (London: SCM Press Ltd, 1982), 95.

[76] Nevertheless, we should not omit Jesus' strong words about the need to fear God instead of man in Luke 12:4,5. Also in her song Mary refers to those who fear God (Luke 1:50). Also, Peter and Paul used the term (Acts 10:34, 35; 2 Cor. 5:11; 2 Cor. 7:1; Col. 3:22; 1 Peter 1:17–19). The early church was described as those who fear the Lord. (Acts 9:31) The eternal gospel proclaimed in Revelation begins with the words: "Fear God and give Him glory ..." (Rev. 14:6,7).

[77] Curtis, Edward M., John J. Brugaletta, *Discovering the Way of Wisdom.* (Grand Rapids: Kregel Publications, 2004), 135.

Some say that being 'filled with the Holy Spirit', a term that is found in the New Testament regularly, expresses a similar reality as 'fearing the Lord'.[78]

The fear of the LORD is a proper perspective

The fear of the LORD encompasses an understanding and perspective of who God is and who we are. Fearing God means to take Him seriously.

> Do not be wise in your own eyes, fear the LORD ... (3:7)

The fear of the LORD saturates our self-evaluation.[79] Fearing God means that we realize we are under authority, that our life is a gift, that we are not the owner, but the steward. Fearing God means to acknowledge our dependence upon Him and "to live all of life in conscious dependence on God."[80] The person who fears God not only acknowledges his or her dependence on God but finds immense joy in such dependence.

The fear of the LORD is 'the renouncing of autonomy and trusting acknowledgment of the Lord at every step of one's practical or intellectual progress.[81] "The God-fearer does not overestimate himself and feel self-confident ..."[82]

Such a proper perspective includes *humility.* Those who fear God know their place in the cosmos. It should therefore be no surprise that in the book of Proverbs humility and fear of the LORD are parallel terms,[83] because humility is the hallmark of those who fear the LORD.

> Humility and fear for Yahweh are made equivalent. Both are interchangeable; one cannot be truly humble without fearing Yahweh; and one cannot fear Yahweh without being truly humble ... The two terms explain and condition each other. A humility that is not centered on fear of Yahweh – and thus submission to His person and revealed will – is a false humility. A professed fear of Yahweh that is not characterized

---

[78]　"Because the Holy Spirit was given in a heightened way through Christ, it would be an overgeneralization to say that the fear of God in the OT was identical to the fullness of the Spirit in the New. Nevertheless, they are describing the same basic reality." (Notes on page 256, 257, in Tim Keller's book The Meaning of Marriage.

[79]　Woodcock, 51–59.

[80]　Bridges, Jerry. *The Joy of Fearing God.* (Colorado: Waterbrook Press, 1997), 192.

[81]　Blocher quoted in *Discovering the Way of Wisdom* – Curtis and Brugaletta, 128.

[82]　Waltke, 595.

[83]　See Proverbs 15:33; 22:4; 28:14.

> by real humility before Him is a false religion. We learn here the important lesson that humility does not arise from thinking less of myself than I ought, but from thinking as much of God as I ought ... This humility is a vital component in fearing Yahweh.[84]

The fear of the LORD is not just an emotion but an attitude, a mindset, a focus of the heart that is very characteristic of the way the relationship between man and God is described in the Bible. It is an attitude that God desires to see in us. A popular definition of the fear of the LORD is "reverential awe."[85]

Fear is a natural result when the Almighty, Sovereign Creator of the universe reveals Himself in power and majesty. Whenever this happened the believers were frightened and terrified. Can you blame them? Who would not fear when one becomes aware of the enormous difference between the Creator and the creature, between the Almighty One and the finite one? When God reveals His power and holiness, we, human beings, sense our own finiteness and unworthiness in the presence of a holy, righteous God. Nevertheless, the fear of God has far more aspects than just the emotion of fear.

The fear of the LORD is a vital relationship

The fear of the LORD is "that filial relationship which, in the most positive senses, puts us securely in our place, and God in His."[86]

> The fear of the LORD is the beginning of wisdom and knowledge of the Holy One is understanding. (9:10)

There is a close connection between 'fearing the LORD' and 'knowing the Holy One.'[87] The word 'knowledge' refers to a personal and intimate relationship with God, the Creator. "This is a fear that clings, rather than recoils."[88]

The fear of the LORD therefore not only describes the distance between God and man, but paradoxically, also the intimate relationship between God and man. How can this be? How can a small, dependent, insignificant, and sinful, creature, have an intimate relationship with the Sovereign, Holy, and Sinless

---

[84]   Phillips, Dan, *God's Wisdom in Proverbs, Hearing God's voice in Scripture*, (The Woodlands: Kress Biblical Resources, 2011), 79–81.

[85]   Bridges, 18.

[86]   Kidner, Derek. *Ezra & Nehemiah* (Downers Grove: Inter Varsity Press, 1979), 113.

[87]   The same truth is stated in other verses in Proverbs, such as 1:7; 2:5 and 30:3.

[88]   Phillips, 86.

God? Only when the Holy and Righteous God forgives our sins and shortcomings. This is exactly the question the Psalmist struggled with.

> "If you, LORD, kept a record of sins, Lord, who could stand? But with you there is forgiveness, so that we can, with reverence, serve you." (Psalm 130:3,4)

Forgiveness bridges the gap between the Fearful and Awesome God and weak and insignificant human beings. This act of forgiveness from God enables us to live near Him, which is here described as reverence (fear) of God. Forgiveness makes it possible that fear of God combines awe and intimacy.

The fear of the LORD, which is the foundation of wisdom, describes an attitude that keeps a perfect balance in our relationship with God. It describes: Being **A**fraid of God and being **A**ttracted to Him; full of **A**we of Him and **A**ffection for Him; being **D**ependent upon God and being **D**evoted to God; being **C**onsumed by His glory and entering His presence with **C**onfidence. The fear of God is an attitude in which we realize God is **I**ncomprehensible, nevertheless, we have can have **I**ntimate relationship with Him. It is an attitude that balances **R**espect of God with **R**ejoicing in Him; in which **M**eekness and **M**ajesty, **T**error and **T**rust coincide.

The fear of the LORD combines the reverential awe which creatures owe to the Highest One and the affection a child has for its father.

> What God is inspires awe; what God has done for His people commands affection. See here the centrifugal and centripetal forces of the moral world, holding the creature reverently distant from the Creator, yet compassing the child about with everlasting love, to keep him near a Father in heaven. The whole of this complicated and reciprocal relation is often indicated in Scriptures by the brief expression, "The fear of the Lord."[89]

The fear of the LORD can be described with a paradoxical phrase as 'An intimate relationship with a consuming fire.'

The fear of the LORD refers to a paradox because it includes concepts such as distance, incomprehensible, awe, holiness, even terror, but at the same time speaks of intimacy, connectedness (loyalty), love, obedience, reverence. God, who is described as a consuming fire is at the same time a Person Whom we

---

[89]　Woodcock, 60.

can relate to intimately. Carefulness and confidentiality go hand in hand. The Fearful One is also the Fully trustworthy One. He is both Judge and Savior.

The fear of the LORD is an expression that best describes what true religion really is. Being religious is not primarily adhering to a set of doctrines, belonging to a religious community, not even performing religious activities, but whether one fears God in the way described above.

The fear of the LORD is a necessary choice

The fear of the LORD is not only a proper perspective and an intimate relationship, but also a mindset, a choice.

We have seen that in the book of Proverbs, Wisdom is metaphorically presented as a woman, who publicly invites people to respond to her and become wise.[90]

Whereas some people accept her invitations, others reject her offer.

> But since you refuse to listen when I call and no one pays attention when I stretch out my hand … (1:24)

When these people begin to experience the consequences of their choice, they cry out to Wisdom to help them. Wisdom refuses to help.

> Then they will call to me but I will not answer; they will look for me but will not find me, since they hated knowledge and did not choose to fear the Lord … (1:28,29)

The attitude of fearing God does not automatically become part of us, nor will it automatically grow in us. It is a mindset we continually need to choose to walk in.

Let not your heart envy sinners but continue in the fear of the LORD all the day. (Proverbs 23:17)

This sometimes means doing certain things simply because God says they are right or abstaining from certain things simply because God abhors these. Sometimes choosing the fear of the LORD means doing what God states is right, despite the enormous pressure from people around us to do otherwise.

---

[90]   see Proverbs 1:20–33; 8; 9:1–12.

How is the fear of the LORD expressed?

We have seen that the fear of the LORD is considered the beginning, the essence and controlling principle of wisdom. We've learned that it refers to an intimate relationship with the awesome Creator. When one has such a relationship this will have practical consequences in daily life. In the book of Proverbs, the fear of the LORD is considered the motivating impulse for our obedience, for all our right acting and right thinking. Fearing the Lord extends to cover a most extensive range of activities and attitudes. It represents a way of life.

First, it is expressed in an attitude of *humility.* We have already seen that in the book of Proverbs humility and fear of God stand in synonymous parallelism.[91]

> The fear of the Lord in the book of Proverbs is the humble, dependable submission to God, that makes him regard God highly and reckons with Him every moment.[92]

We can recognize someone that is humble by his or her willingness to be open to correction, to learn from others. We will look at this in more detail later in this book.

Secondly, our fear of the LORD is also expressed in our *obedience* to the words, precepts, and commands of God. We fear God by obeying Him.

The fear of the LORD is also seen in one's *moral life.* The book of Proverbs makes a strong link between the fear of the Lord and one's moral life.

> The wise fear the LORD and shun evil" (14:16).[93]

In the book of Proverbs "it is the ethical aspect of the fear of the Lord that is most prominent."[94]

The fear of the LORD, which "is approximately equivalent to "piety" appears in the book of Proverbs as a set phrase denoting the totality of the righteous man's life-style."[95]

---

[91] Proverbs 15:33; 22:4; 28:14.

[92] Oosterhoff, B.J. *De Vreze des HEREN in het Oude Testament.* (Utrecht: Kemink en Zoon, 1949), 87.

[93] See also Proverbs 3:7; 14:2; 16:6; 8:13.

[94] Whybray, 36.

The fear of the LORD is considered the basis for *upright conduct*. The one who fears the LORD "walks uprightly." (14:2). He who fears the LORD walks in straight paths, he or she is honest in his dealings with others and will not seek personal gain by dishonestly causing damage to others. He or she is a good citizen.[96]

In the last chapter of Proverbs, we get a good description about what it means for a married woman to fear the LORD in her day-to-day life. She seeks the good of her family and others and considers her welfare not for self-indulgence but as a possibility to widen her responsibilities. She is a tireless worker, who pays the people she is responsible for, a fair wage and she uses her means to help the poor.[97]

The fear of the LORD results in *developing God-like attitudes in dealing with people and circumstances.* Love and fidelity, two concepts that are often mentioned as characteristics of the Lord, are mentioned as characteristics of those who fear God.[98] Here it is used to refer to relationship with others. Fearing the LORD results in developing God-like attitudes in dealing with people and circumstances.

The fear of the LORD *motivates right behavior* even when socially enforced sanctions do not exist or cannot be effective, because the person who fears God wants to reflect the character of the one, true, living God. It is an affectionate reverence that results in humbly bowing to God's will. It is a desire not to sin against Him because His wrath is so awful, and His love is so formidable.

The opposite of fearing the LORD is despising Him. This despising may be unconscious, but nevertheless real. *"Every departure from God's path is a backing of one's judgment, against His."*[99]

The benefits of the fear of the LORD

When we want to become a wise person, we must develop the attitude of fearing God. While we grow into a person that fears the LORD, we will grow

---

[95] Boström, L. *The God of the Sages: The Portrayal of God in the Book of Proverbs.* (Stockholm: Almqvist & Wiksell, 1990), 101.

[96] See Proverbs 8:13; 10:27; 14:2; 14:16; 14:27; 15:16; 16:6; 23:17,18; 24:21; 28:14.

[97] Proverbs 31:10–31.

[98] Proverbs 16:6 In Ex. 34:6 these characteristics are mentioned as characteristics of God.

[99] Kidner, Proverbs, 106.

into becoming a wise father, mother, daughter, son, colleague, citizen etc. This will benefit the people whom we live and work with and society at large. The book of Proverbs also points out that the fear of the LORD is 'a beneficial therapy'[100] not only for society at large, but also for the people that fear the LORD. Growing into a person that fears God will bring some important benefits, such as: health, hope, security, life, wealth, honour, and contentment.[101] We might experience some of these benefits, or blessings temporarily, already in this live, while others will be fulfilled in the eternal live to come.

Nevertheless, it is important to not seek these benefits as a motive for fearing the LORD, nor to lose sight of the fact that spiritual and moral values are considered worthier than physical values.

> Although the sage value earthly happiness, this in the end is not the most important. That becomes clear when he speaks about richness. On the hand he sees richness as a fruit of wisdom and fear of the Lord … on the other hand he points out that it is less important than spiritual and moral values … and can even be dangerous … This also becomes clear from the prayer of Agur … Richness and earthly happiness in themselves are worthless for the sage, he believes that it is better to have "a little with the fear of the Lord than great wealth with turmoil." (15:16)[102]

This beginning of wisdom will have a profound influence on the way we walk, talk, choose our friends, use our money, spend … as we will see in the next chapters.

Conclusion

Having looked at the phrase 'the fear of the LORD' as it was known to Solomon, we begin to understand why he considers this kind of relationship of holy regard, trust, and submission to God foundational in his quest for wisdom. Without this foundational attitude our pursuit of wisdom will not bring us to true wisdom that is characteristically humble, but will lead to arrogance and self-righteousness, someone who is impressed with his own wisdom. In fact,

---

[100] McKane, William. *Proverbs*. Old Testament Library. (Philadelphia: Westminster, 1970), 293.

[101] Proverbs 3:7,8; 23:17,18; 10:27; 14:26,27; 22:4; 15:16; 19:23.

[102] Oosterhoff, 121.

such people are described as fools. *If anyone holds God in contempt, he will never be a wise person.*[103]

Without a vital relationship with God, which is expressed in the phrase 'fear of the LORD', no one could possibly attain enough wisdom to merit the adjective "wise." The fear of the LORD is both the source as well as the motive for acquiring wisdom. Fear of God is both the foundation and the result of wisdom. The fear of the LORD stands both at the beginning of our quest for wisdom and is also one of the characteristics of a wise person.

Questions for further reflection

1. Explain why you (dis)agree with the description of the fear of God as 'an intimate relationship with a consuming fire.'

2. What image would best describe your relationship with God?

3. How would you define a God-fearing person?

---

[103] Anders, 15.

CHAPTER 4
HOW TO BECOME WISE?

Then you will understand what is right and just and fair—every good path.
For wisdom will enter your heart, and knowledge will be pleasant to your soul.
Discretion will protect you, and understanding will guard you.
Proverbs 2:9–11

A lesson from gold-digging

People have been digging for gold for thousands of years. A group of German and Georgian archaeologists claims the Sakdrisi site in southern Georgia, dating to the 3rd or 4th millennium B.C., may be the world's oldest known gold mine.[104] During the 19th century, numerous gold rushes in remote regions around the globe caused large migrations of miners, such as the California Gold Rush of 1849, the Victorian Gold Rush, and the Klondike Gold Rush. The discovery of gold in the Witwatersrand led to the Second Boer War and the founding of South Africa. The high price of gold has inspired thousands of people to become amateur prospectors. Many of them are spending their weekends or vacations in search of the yellow metal.

While discovering gold is an exciting prospect, becoming a gold prospector takes quite a lot of preparation, determination, and perseverance.

One must *acquire knowledge*, such as: where gold has been found in the past; where one can legally prospect; what are the local prospecting laws and regulations; background information on gold deposits and geology.

One has *to develop skills* (e.g. to transfer property boundaries to maps or GPS devices for easy use in the field; to use a metal detector; to have metal detecting techniques; to have a basic geology of gold and rock recognition; to know how to set up and use of Geomap on one's computer with basic GPS understanding; to know what to do after one finds gold, to know how to cleans it and how to sell it).

---

[104] https://en.wikipedia.org/wiki/Gold_mining.

One has the option to attend a three-day Gold Prospecting Training[105] or join a prospecting club.

One must *do research and obtaining permissions* into areas where gold might be found. These might be areas that historically have produced gold. Once decided on where to search one must find out who owns the land, contact the owner, ask permission from the owner of the land one wants to search for gold, which includes informing them how anything found will be reported and shared with the landowner.

Then one must *determine which method* one wants to use: placer mining, panning, sluicing, dredging, rocker box, hard rock mining. The method one wants to use influences the *equipment* one needs *to purchase*, such as: a gold pan, a sieve, a metal detector, a rock tumbler, a woodman's pal machete, protective material against snake bites, a GPS, a shovel, a vibrating gold classifier, a suction dredge, a sluice, a gold cube etc.

Then if one is lucky, one finds gold, like John R. Wilsdon:

> Been gold prospecting for 7 years, mainly in the Bradshaw Mountains, Yavapai, Arizona. Found over eight grams of placer.[106]

In an article, entitled "Prospecting for Gold in the United States" on the website of the United States Geological Survey, Harold Kirkemo, Chief of the Office of Minerals Exploration writes "There are few thrills comparable to finding gold." Nevertheless, those that jump into the gold rush, he cautions:

> Some degree of success in finding gold still remains for those choosing favorable areas after a careful study of mining records and the geology of the mining districts. Serious prospecting should not be attempted by anyone without sufficient capital to support a long and possibly discouraging campaign of preliminary work. The prospective gold seeker must have ample funds to travel to and from the region he selects to prospect and to support the venture. He must be prepared to undergo physical hardships, possess a car capable of traveling the roughest and steepest roads, and not be discouraged by repeated disappointments.

---

[105] http://www.gold-prospecting-wa.com/gold-prospecting-lessons-cue.html.

[106] https://owlcation.com/misc/Where-to-Find-Gold-if-You-are-a-Newbie-Gold-Prospe cting-the-Best-Places-Using-Gold-Panning.

Even if a discovery of value is not found, the venture will have been interesting and challenging.[107]

The preparation, research, developing skills, using tools needed to dig for gold serves as an illustration to stimulate us in our quest for wisdom. Although gold is valuable, wisdom is more valuable.

How much better to get wisdom than gold … (16:16).

While only a few of those who search for gold are successful, the success rate for those seeking wisdom is hundred percent.

… those who diligently seek me will find me. (8:17)

What are the necessary steps that we need to take in our quest for wisdom?

We have already seen that we need to start off from the right **foundation**: the fear of the LORD. While having this mindset is necessary to make sure that we take the right path, to arrive at our destination, we need to take some additional steps and we need tools and equipment.

Let us start to clarify our **destination**. Well, you say: isn't that clear? We have been talking about our quest for wisdom all along, so our destination is wisdom. Yes, but wisdom is not abstract. It is not something that we can hold in our hands, it is not something we can see as an object. Our quest for wisdom really should mean that we want wisdom in our hearts, in the control room of our life, influencing all our decisions, guiding all our words and actions. We want wisdom to become part of our character, our personality. Our quest for wisdom is only completed when wisdom has come into our hearts.

How does it get there? It is important that we realize that from a Biblical perspective, wisdom is **a divine gift**. It is something that God bestows on those who fear Him. The source of wisdom is divine revelation. Nevertheless, one is not simply to pray and wait for God to download wisdom into our hearts. It does take arduous work.

Before we move on in our quest, we must do some deep **soul-searching**. Do I really want to have wisdom? Really? With my whole being, with my total commitment? Am I willing to go to a great length to get it? Am I willing to suffer hardships to get it? Am I willing to go to the same trouble to get wisdom as

---

[107] https://pubs.usgs.gov/gip/prospect2/prospectgip.html.

people have gone to look for gold or silver or hidden treasure? Among other things, they were willing to suffer sickness, cold/heat, lack of sanitation, loneliness, starvation. We must commit ourselves to the pursuit of wisdom.

> Wisdom is hard to gain even after you have given yourself to it. It is impossible without commitment to it.[108]

Cultivating wisdom is a deliberate choice that people can make regardless of age and intelligence.

Paul Baltes, a German psychologist, who has written extensively about wisdom from a scientific point of view, mentions three conditions that are relevant for the development of wisdom:

> Three life conditions are particularly relevant for the development of wisdom: extensive experience with a wide range of human conditions; tutor- or mentor-guided practice; and motivational dispositions such as generativity (Erikson, 1959) or the continuing motivation to expand one's insights into matters of life and their mastery (Brim, 1992; Ryff, 1989a, 1989b) Under such enhancing conditions, it seems in principle possible that growing old harbors the opportunity for growth in the bodies of knowledge that we call wisdom.[109]

He does not take into consideration that to become wise is not only demanding work but also a divine gift, which requires not just an ardent search but also a receptive spirit.

> My son, if you accept my words and store up my commands within you, turning your ear to wisdom and applying your heart to understanding – indeed if you call out for insight and cry aloud for understanding, and if you look for it as for silver and search for it as for hidden treasure, then you will understand the fear of the Lord and find the knowledge of God. For the Lord gives wisdom; from his mouth come knowledge and understanding. He holds success in store for the upright, he is a shield to those whose walk is blameless, for he guards the course of the just and protects the way of his faithful ones. Then you will understand what is right and just and fair – every good path. For wisdom will enter your

---

[108] Anders, 17.

[109] Baltes P.B., Smith J., Staudinger U.M. "Wisdom and successful aging." 123–167 in Sonderegger (Ed), *Psychology and Aging*; Nebraska Symposium on Motivation, 1991.

> heart, and knowledge will be pleasant to your soul. Discretion will protect you, and understanding will guard you. (Proverbs 2:1–11)

To get wisdom, we need to turn our ear, apply our heart, call out, look for and search. This passage speaks of a determination, and a commitment on our part. A fervent desire that says: "I desperately want wisdom no matter what it takes." We need to seek it with the same urgent passion as we might look for a hidden treasure.

> "… Like any expertise, the acquisition and refinement of wisdom involves an extended and intense process of learning, practice, as well as the motivation to strive toward excellence."[110]

The book of Proverbs makes clear that God gives wisdom, knowledge and understanding to the upright, the blameless and the faithful ones. While prayer that God will grant us wisdom is one of the first steps to become a wise person, it is by no means the last or only step. But, as a Chinese wisdom proverb says, "Even a very long journey begins with a single step."

The book of Proverbs gives us several suggestions on how to become wise.

Cultivate the fear of the LORD

In the previous chapter we have seen that from a Biblical perspective, the essence of wisdom is 'the fear of the LORD'. We learned there that if we one wants to gain wisdom as the Bible defines it, one must start with developing a fear of God. Without the fear of the LORD, one cannot acquire true wisdom. Because fearing the LORD is an essential prerequisite for becoming wise, it is important for those who want to become wise to cultivate this attitude in our lives. We will not grow in the fear of the LORD unless we work at it.

Jerry Bridges gives helpful suggestions to help us grow in the fear of the LORD:

- Read about His mighty acts performed in the past as recorded in the Scriptures and other books.

- Reflect about His immense greatness as seen in creation and history.

---

[110] Baltes, P.B. & Staudinger, U.M. (2000). "Wisdom: A metaheuristic (pragmatic) to orchestrate mind and virtue toward excellence." *American Psychologist*, 55(1), 122–136.

- Cherish His greatness, grandeur, excellence, and perfection as revealed to us both in His Word and His works. Develop a habit of thinking great thoughts about God.

- Develop an ever-deepening awareness of His holiness and transcendent majesty.

- Admire His sovereign and manifold wisdom.

- Worship His amazing love and grace. You grow in the fear of God by gazing upon the beauty of His attributes and by seeking an ever-deepening relationship with Him.[111]

Learn from life

For individuals to develop wisdom, they must be willing to learn from life.

> The development of wisdom does not depend on *what* kind of events people encounter in life but on *how* they deal with those events … It appears that wisdom can only be obtained if people are willing to accept the lessons that life has to offer and to be transformed in the process.[112]

Wisdom is gained through experiences, but only if people are willing to examine life experiences and learn and apply the lessons that life has to offer them. This means we need: to regard, to reflect, to respond and to remember.

To regard

To become wise, one needs to learn from creation and experience. We need to take time to regard and observe life around us, be it ants or the condition of our flocks.

> Go to the ant, you sluggard; consider its ways and be wise (6:6)

Be sure you know the condition of your flocks, give careful attention to your herd. (27:23)

We can observe what are the consequences of marital unfaithfulness, of being a sluggard, how the household of a woman who fears God functions, what

---

[111] Bridges, 255.

[112] Ardelt, M. "Being wise at any age." In Shane J. Lopez (Ed.): *Positive psychology: Exploring the best in people. Volume 1: Discovering human strengths* (Westport, C.T.: Praeger, 2008), 81–108.

happens to those skilled in work; the havoc caused by alcohol; the beauty and order of creation as a reflection of the wisdom of the Creator.[113]

> At the window of my house I *looked down* … I *saw* among the simple, I *noticed* among the young men, a youth who had no sense. He was going down the street near her corner, walking along in the direction of her house at twilight as the day was fading as the dark night set in … (7:6–9)

> I went past the field of a sluggard, past the vineyard of someone who has no sense; thorns had come up everywhere, the ground was covered with weeds. (24:30,31)

> *Do you see someone* skilled in their work? They will serve before kings; they will not serve before officials of low rank. (22:29)

The strategy of the sage is to provide youth with opportunities to observe experiences at a distance without having to pay the consequences of irresponsible behavior … Exposing youth to experiences they can observe in others is a form of inoculation, a powerful means of "receiving instruction" (24:32) … For the sage, then, instruction occurs in observing life.[114]

To reflect

Then I saw and considered it; I looked and received instruction. (Proverbs 24:32, ESV)

Observing and regarding should lead to reflection. Learning from life involves reflection, integration, and application. Reflection and integration mean taking in and processing information.

> In a loose series of conscious or unconscious actions (e.g., writing, talking, or thinking), students process information gained from experiences and interactions and transform them into something more meaningful: analyzing (separating the information into parts, then considering the information in new ways); connecting (between new information and existing areas in one's life); contextualizing (associating the similarities

---

[113] The household of a woman who fears the Lord (31:10–31); The havoc caused by alcohol (23:29–35); The beauty and order of creation as a reflection of the wisdom of the Creator (3:19,20; 8).

[114] Bland, Dave, "The Formation of Character in the Book of Proverbs." *Restoration Quarterly* 40.4 (1998), 221–237.

and dissimilarities between the new information and previous knowledge); and synthesizing (bringing the new information into the existing knowledge, creating a new whole)."[115]

Once we have engaged in reflection and integration, application can take place. This could mean we make changes in our attitudes, values, behavior, opinions, options, or plans.

To respond

The regarding and reflecting should result in responding. Learning from life also includes learning from our mistakes and to learn from reproof or rebuke from others, irrespective whether such reproof comes from a friend or a foe. A good reproof is a work of art.

> Like gold or an ornament of gold is a wise reproof to a listening ear. (25:12).

But even if others are not using a sophisticated version of a rebuke, we do well to pay attention.

> Whoever heeds life-giving correction will be at home among the wise. Those who disregard discipline despise themselves, but the one who heeds correction gains understanding." (15:31,32)[116]

We also need to respond to the teaching that we receive from parents, teachers, and other wise people that we meet.

Listen, my sons to a father's instruction; pay attention and gain understanding. (4:1)

The wise in heart accept commands, but a chattering fool comes to ruin. (10:8)

Listen to advice and accept discipline and at the end you will be counted among the wise. (19:20)

Pay attention and turn your ear to the sayings of the wise, apply your heart to what I teach ... (22:17)

---

[115] Brown, S.C." Learning across the campus: How college facilitates the development of wisdom". *Journal of College Student Development*, 2004, 45(2), 134–148.

[116] Other verses that express a similar thought: Proverbs 9:8,9; 10:17; 12:1; 13:18; 15:5,12; 17:10; 19:20,25; 29:15.

To remember

Having learned from the lessons of life by regarding, reflecting, and responding, it is of course of utmost importance that what we have learned becomes part of our lives. To remember our lessons from life, we can write them down, or make them part of our life' purpose statement. This can help us to develop these lessons into our habits, which will shape our character.

In the book of Proverbs, we find a lot of short sentences drawn from long experiences. The book regularly exhorts the readers to bind the instructions on our fingers, and around our neck and to write them on our heart and have them ready on our lips.[117] To help us do this, many of the lessons are written in powerful one-liners.[118]

> These instructions are packaged in the memorable form of the proverb. Parallelism enables the proverb to be tucked away easily into the corners of the mind ready for active duty when the occasion arises. Proverbs make instructions portable.[119]

To grow in wisdom, we need to learn from live by reflecting on our experiences, regarding the world outside, responding to reproof and remembering all these lessons, because:

> What distinguish wise people from intelligent/knowledgeable individuals are not their cognitive abilities but their capacity for self-reflection and self-transformation … Wisdom is knowledge that is realized through experiences, self-reflection, and self-examination by listening to the lessons that life offers.[120]

Associate with the right kind of people

He who walks with wise men will be wise, but the companion of fools will be destroyed. (13:30)

---

[117] Proverbs 1:9; 3:3; 7:3; 22:17,18.

[118] A warning is necessary: simply learning these one-liners by heart does not make you a wise person, see the warnings in Proverbs 26:7,9.

[119] Bland, Dave, "The Formation of Character in the Book of Proverbs." *Restoration Quarterly* 40.4 (1998), 221–237.

[120] Ardelt, M. Being wise at any age. In Shane J. Lopez (Ed.): *Positive psychology: Exploring the best in people. Volume 1: Discovering human strengths.* Westport, C.T.: Praeger, 2008), 81–108.

To be become wise we not only need to cultivate the fear of God, and learn from life in its various dimensions, but we also need to associate with the right kind of people.

> One of the oldest means of acquiring wisdom is through observation and emulation. It is in this sense that wise people of the past are remembered and held up as examples, as are people we admire in our own life … Historical accounts of developing wisdom are often accounts of mentoring or apprenticeship.[121]

> As with any other high-level expertise, guidance by mentors or other wisdom-enhancing "voices" of society as well as the experience and mastery of critical life experiences are likely necessary.[122]

One can associate' with people, by spending time with them, or by reading about/from them. Written biographies can be considered as historical mentors.

Psychologist Jonathan Haidt, compiled the following wisdom-building activities:

- Read the works of great thinkers and religious leaders (e.g., Gandhi, Buddha, Jesus, Mother Theresa, Nelson Mandela). Read classic works of literature. Contemplate the wisdom of the ages.

- Think of the wisest person you know. Try to live each day as that person would live.

- Look up prominent people in history and learn their views on important issues of their day.

- Volunteer at a nursing home and talk with residents about their lives and the lessons they have learned.[123]

---

[121] Ferrari, M. "Developing Expert and Transformative Wisdom Developing Expert and Transformative Wisdom: Can Either Be Taught in Public Schools?" Ferrari, Michel, and Georges Potworowski (eds.) *Teaching for Wisdom: Cross-Cultural Perspectives on Fostering Wisdom.* (New York: Springer, 2008).

[122] Baltes, P.B. & Staudinger, U.M. "Wisdom: A metaheuristic (pragmatic) to orchestrate mind and virtue toward excellence." *American Psychologist*, 55(1), 2000, 122–136.

[123] In his article "Finding Phronimos: Making a Place for Practical Wisdom in the Classroom", Corwynn Beals, describes how he gave his students the following assign-

- Subscribe to two news editorial publications that are on opposite ends of the political spectrum … Read them both and consider both sides of the issues.[124]

One way to associate with the right kind of people is to seek out a wise person to be your mentor.

The way of the fool seems right to them, but the wise listen to advice. (Proverbs 12:15)

Although life experiences remain the key for the acquisition of wisdom, a wise mentor can serve as a guide through those experiences.

While all of this is valuable, it is important to keep in mind that without fear of the Lord there is no real foundation to wisdom. In the Bible we find several life stories of men and women who were wise based on their fear of the Lord. For example, the life of Joseph, about whom it is said 'there is no one so discerning and wise as you' (Genesis 41:39), or Daniel, of whom we read 'Daniel spoke to him with wisdom and tact' (Daniel 2:14).

One of the clearest examples of a wise person, is of course Jesus Christ, who is the ultimate embodiment of God's wisdom:

> My goal is that they may be encouraged in heart and united in love, so that they may have the full riches of complete understanding, in order that they may know the mystery of God, namely Christ, in whom are hidden all the treasures of wisdom and knowledge. (Colossians 2: 2,3)

To avail of His wisdom, one needs to live in a close relationship with Him and be familiar with His life and words.

---

ment: 1) Find a person over the age of 62 whom you respect and admire-someone whom it might even be apt to describe as "wise." 2) Spend at least two hours with this person, preferably over two or three separate meetings 3) During the course of your conversation, try to glean some wisdom from him or her; 4) Try doing this by asking questions (he gave them questions; 5) Write a 400–500-word summary of your conversation along with your assessment of the experience. For more information: see Beals, Corwynn, "Finding Phronimos: Making a Place for Practical Wisdom in the Classroom" (2004), Faculty Publications – College of Christian Studies. 135. https://digitalcommons.georgefox.edu/ccs/135.

[124] Referred to by Ben Dean in his article on Wisdom; https://www.authentichappiness.sas.upenn.edu/newsletters/authentichappinesscoaching/wisdom.

The older, the wiser?

> "According to the researchers, 60 is the optimal age for possessing wisdom."[125]

Cultivating the fear of the Lord and learning from life by regarding, reflecting, responding, and remembering, and associating with the right kind of people helps us to become a wise person. Considering this, it is natural to assume that the older one gets the wiser one becomes.

> Intellectual knowledge can be learned early in life through all kinds of media, whereas the acquisition of wisdom requires learning from life itself through individual experiences, which is likely to take more time.[126]

Nevertheless, one is not wise because one is old, nor does one automatically become wise because one grows old.

> One can be old and foolish, but a wise man is likely to be old, simply because such growth takes time.[127]

It is also possible to find wisdom in younger people, particularly those who have become wise by dealing with hardships in their life, such as serious health or family problems.[128]

In the Bible we find young men and women who behave in a wise manner, e.g., Joseph, Ruth, Daniel, and Jesus. We also find young men sometimes be wiser than older men (e.g., Elihu, who listened to Job's friends and rebukes them, Job 32:6–9). We also have examples in the Bible of men who were wise while younger, but became foolish later in life (e.g. Adam, Solomon).

Having said this, under normal circumstances, the elderly have wisdom.

---

[125] Targowski, Andrew. "Teaching for Wisdom." *Dialogue and Universalism*, Volume 22, issue 3, 2012, 93–114.

[126] Ardelt, M. "Being wise at any age." In Shane J. Lopez (Ed.): *Positive psychology: Exploring the best in people. Volume 1: Discovering human strengths* (Westport, CT: Praeger, 2008), 81–108.

[127] Kekes, John. "Wisdom", *American Philosophical Quarterly*, 20:3 (July 1983), 286.

[128] Ardelt, M. "Being wise at any age." In Shane J. Lopez (Ed.): *Positive psychology: Exploring the best in people. Volume 1: Discovering human strengths* (Westport, CT: Praeger, 2008), 97.

The relation between wisdom and age is *potentially* positive if the individual remains willing to learn from experiences and to engage in self-reflection and self-examination.[129]

Can one teach wisdom in a school?

The book of Proverbs gives a perspective on the efforts of a religious community to educate its youth in becoming wise people. There is no clear indication that this education took place in school.

> For wisdom the household had become both a school and a spiritual training ground. In spite of clues which may point to the existence of schools in Israel, the primary responsibility for instruction in the book of Proverbs falls on the family. A home, not a school, is the *literary* milieu of Proverbs.[130]

In modern times both families and schools are responsible to prepare our youth to become mature adults. Education typically focuses on imparting content knowledge and developing cognitive skills in the students. We have already seen that intellectual knowledge is different from wisdom. People can be highly intelligent, but that does not necessarily mean they are wise. While intellectual knowledge can be learned in school, this does not seem to be true for wisdom, which as we have seen is acquired through firsthand experiences and other elements mentioned above.

Aristotle thought that practical wisdom was not something that could be taught as knowledge is taught.[131]

Nevertheless, recently the question has been asked whether schools can develop a curriculum in having the students grow in wisdom. Some scholars argue that schools and universities should not only teach intellectual knowledge but also promote the development of wisdom so that individuals at any age will have the chance to be wise and to benefit from their wisdom throughout their life.

---

[129] Ibid, 96.

[130] Bland, Dave, "The Formation of Character in the Book of Proverbs" *Restoration Quarterly* 40.4 (1998) 221–237, page 225, 226.

[131] "Practical wisdom cannot be knowledge nor art; not knowledge, because that which can be done is capable of being otherwise, not art because action and making are different kinds of thing." NE, IIK VI, 1140b2–5.

Corey Beals, Assistant Professor of Religious Studies at George Fox University in Newberg wanted to encourage the development of practical wisdom among his students, by giving them one assignment:

> I required that my students find a *phronimos* (someone of advanced age whom they considered to have a high degree of practical wisdom) and engage this person in at least two hours of conversation, preferably over more than one encounter. I provided the students with a list of possible starter questions to get their phronimos talking. They were then required to write a summary of the conversation(s) and their assessment of the experience.[132]

Professor Andrew Targowski of Haworth College of Business Western Michigan University believes that the basic aim of education should be to learn how to acquire wisdom in life. As a result, he developed and taught an interdisciplinary course on Wisdom at Western Michigan University in 2012. This course was in his own words "the first formal course on wisdom at Western Michigan University and perhaps in the whole United States."

> This course will investigate inter-disciplinary approaches to wisdom, such as philosophical, conventional, cognitive, civilizational, political, and other. As the result of this course the student should have conceptual knowledge and analytical skills to apply wisdom in his/her private and professional life.

> After completing this course students should be able to: Recognize, analyze, and suggest various types of live situations based on wisdom-based strategy; Integrate data, information, concept, knowledge, and wisdom into thinking, reasoning and action, Identify main pillars of wisdom such as; emotion, knowing what is important, moral reasoning, compassion, humility, altruism, patience, dealing with uncertainty, prudence, within a big-picture conceptualization, worldliness, morality (ethics), tolerance, understanding, methods, dialogue, practicality, and so forth.[133]

---

[132] Beals, Corwynn, "Finding Phronimos: Making a Place for Practical Wisdom in the Classroom" (2004). Faculty Publications – College of Christian Studies. 135. https://digitalcommons.georgefox.edu/ccs/135.

[133] Targowski, Andrew. *WISDOM HNRS 4900-Spring 2012*; (Kalamazoo, MI: A. Targowski/Civilization Press, 2012).

Robert Sternberg has developed the program called *Teaching for Wisdom*, which is a curriculum program to help teachers teach for wisdom. This program was designed to facilitate the development of wise and critical thinking skills in middle school children through the infusion of these skills into a history curriculum.[134]

> We believe that the goal of teaching for wisdom can be achieved by providing students with educational contexts where students can formulate their own understanding of what constitutes wise thinking. In other words, teaching for wisdom is not accomplished through a didactic method of 'imparting' information about wisdom and subsequently assessing students with multiple-choice questions. Instead, students need to actively experience various cognitive and affective processes that underlie wise decision making.[135]

Sternberg believes that schools can at least provide the scaffolding for the acquisition of wisdom by teaching students not just *what* to think but also *how* to think.

> I am not advocating a new course called "Wisdom" or some such. I think that the creation of such a new course would indeed be unrealistic and impractical. Rather, I am arguing for the infusion of thinking for wisdom into the curriculum as it now exists.[136]

Scott C. Brown, Director of the Daniel L. Jones Career Development Center at Mount Holyoke developed *Brown's Model of Wisdom Development* for educators in higher education in the US. His model is intended

> to provide educators with a framework for considering how to more purposefully influence the integrative nature of the educational experience to enhance the development of wisdom.[137]

---

[134] Sternberg, Robert J., Linda Jarvin and Alina Reznitskaya, "Teaching for Wisdom Through History: Infusing Wise Thinking Skills in the School Curriculum". In M. Ferrari and G. Potworowski (eds), *Teaching for Wisdom*, 2008.

[135] Ibid.

[136] Sternberg, Robert J. "How Wise Is It to Teach for Wisdom? A Reply to Five Critiques.". *Educational. Psychologist*, 2001, 36:4, 269–272.

[137] Brown, S.C., "Learning across the campus: How college facilitates the development of wisdom". *Journal of College Student Development*, 45(2), 2004, 134–148.

Brown believes that wisdom comprises of six dimensions: self-knowledge, understanding of others, judgment, life knowledge, life skills, and willingness to learn. He believes that

> Wisdom develops when students go through the core "learning-from-life" process, comprised of reflection, integration, and application. The conditions that facilitate the development of wisdom by directly or indirectly stimulating the "learning-from-life" process are the student's (a) orientation to learning, (b) experiences, (c) interactions with others, and (d) environment. Depending on how deeply and how often students were stimulated to go through the learning from life process, they experienced growth on one or more of the six dimensions of wisdom.[138]

Ardelt believes that teaching meditation will help students to grow in wisdom:

> Spiritual practices have been designed to foster the development of wisdom in addition to learning from life experiences … The practice of meditation, in particular, tends to result in self-reflection and self-awareness, a decrease of self-centeredness, greater sympathy and compassion for others, and ultimately greater wisdom (Pascual-Leone, 2000). In fact, teaching meditation to students might be one way to promote the development of wisdom in schools and universities.[139]

While it commendable to seek ways to instruct our children and students in wisdom, the examples given above focus on practical wisdom only, without the necessary Biblical component, which the book of Proverbs calls the foundation of wisdom, namely the fear of the Lord.

Pastor and author Kevin Swanson states that some educational programs "have a semblance of truth, but all will fundamentally be compromised if they do not begin with the book of Proverbs and the fear of God."[140]

He continues:

---

[138] Brown, S.C., Greene, J.A., "The Wisdom Development Scale: translating the conceptual to the concrete." *Journal of College Student Development.* 2008; 47(1):1–19.

[139] Ardelt, M. "Being wise at any age." In Shane J. Lopez (Ed.). *Positive psychology: Exploring the best in people. Volume 1: Discovering human strengths* (Westport, CT: Praeger, 2008), 81–108.

[140] Swanson, Kevin. *The Book of Proverbs: God's Book of Wisdom Book 1.* (Elizabeth, CO: Generations with Vision, 2011).

> The separation of the fear of God from the chemistry class has produced an ungodly, secular science … The separation of the fear of God from social studies and political science has undermined the Christian foundation of this country and created tyranny … Christian teachers who teach chemistry should be less interested in their student learning chemistry as they are in their students learning the fear of God through chemistry … Thus we do not separate discipleship from education or the fear of God from the academic subjects. … Therefore, every teaching college in America … should require its students to memorize the book of Proverbs.[141]

To help children of nine years and older grow in wisdom and the fear of the Lord Swanson developed a *Family Study Bible Guide on the Book of Proverbs.*[142]

> Of all of the possible curriculum choices used for the education of our children, the most important textbook of all is that which God Himself presented in the book of Proverbs. This book is the core curriculum. It is God's book on how to live life on planet earth. To disregard this book in the education of our children would be a colossal error."[143]

To which we could add: not only children, but also adults.

Questions for further reflection

1. How do you cultivate wisdom in your life?

2. What are some of the lessons you have learned in your life that you would like to pass on to the next generation?

3. How often do you take time to reflect on your life and how does this reflection look like?

---

[141] Ibid.

[142] https://store.generations.org/products/proverbs-i-study-guide-1-15?variant=2364 2806467.

[143] https://store.generations.org/products/proverbs-collection-1-2-3.

CHAPTER 5
CHARACTERISTICS OF A WISE PERSON

*From all nations people came to listen to Solomon's wisdom, sent by all the
kings of the world, who had heard of his wisdom.*
1 Kings 4:34

When you ask someone to give some characteristics of a wise person, it is highly
likely you get a variety of answers. The answers may have to do with the one's
cultural, ethnic, professional, or religious background. Also, the question to
name some of the historical or contemporary wise people can lead to a variety
of answers. Some would refer to biblical people like Abraham, Solomon, or Jesus.
Others would name Muhammad or Buddha. Others would more rapidly
think of Gandhi, Mandela, Mother Theresa or their mother or grandfather.

> I consider my mother to be very wise. I go to her when my life gets confusing
> because she always seems to have the right answer. Not only
> does she offer the right answer, but she can offer different solutions
> and the consequences of each of those solutions ... I consider my mother
> to be wise because she has had many various experiences throughout
> her lifetime. And it is because of these experiences that she is able
> to offer me advice to get through my life's experiences. Sometimes the
> answers she provides are solutions that are relatively simple, but I always
> find myself saying "I should have thought of that."[144]

> [One] reason I consider my grandfather to be wise is his composure. He
> is always very even keeled, and I have never honestly seen him get
> worked up about anything. Even at times of absolute joy all one sees is
> a very satisfied smile. I believe that this is an important mark of wisdom
> as he understands that there is always going to be good and bad events
> in one's life and that fussing about it changes nothing. Furthermore, he
> is able to live by this in addition to understanding it. The balance he
> lives his life by is ultimately the reason I consider him to be wise.[145]

Of course, the person someone mentions as being wise has to do with one's
own perception of wisdom and one's cultural background.

---

[144] Ardelt, *Being Wise at Any Age*, 87.
[145] Ibid, 85.

In research among American, Australian, Japanese, and Indian young adults, it became clear that the conceptualization of wisdom in the West differs from that in the East, with the former emphasizing the cognitive dimensions and the latter stressing the affective dimensions. While among those from the West, 'being wise' was most strongly associated with 'being knowledgeable' those from the East perceived ``being wise'' as most strongly associated with `being discreet.'

> Hence, what these findings suggest is that the Indian and Japanese adults were less likely than their Western counterparts to relate ``wise'' with analytical features such as the accumulation of a knowledge database. Instead, the Eastern participants identified ``wise'' with the ``discreet'' characteristic, which requires not only ``knowledge'' but also prudence or exercising sound judgement in a practical and emotional situation. In other words, ``wise'' is conceptualized in the East not as mere analytical ability but as a psychological quality that emphasizes more ``direct'' understanding with a great deal of emotional involvement or an effective integration of multiple aspects of human consciousness (e.g., cognition, affect, intuition, etc.).[146]

As already observed, wisdom has become a growing field of interest not only philosophers, but also among psychologists, theologians, educationalists, and people involved in leadership training. Many of these are interested in finding out what are the characteristics of a wise person. There have been tools developed to measure wisdom, such as the *Three-Dimensional Wisdom Scale*, and the *Self-Assessed Wisdom Scale*; also, *The Wisdom Development Scale* and the *Foundational Value Scale*.[147]

Most people involved in researching wisdom identify cognitive, reflective, and affective characteristics as essential elements of wisdom. Wisdom is seen to be a combination of cognitive, reflective, and affective personality characteristics.

---

[146] Masami Takahashi Masami & Prashant Bordia." The Concept of Wisdom: A Cross-cultural Comparison." *International Journal of Psychology*, 2000 35:1, 1–9.

[147] Ardelt. Others are: Self-Assessed Wisdom-Scale (SAWS) developed by Webster (2003); The Wisdom Development Scale by Scott C. Brown, Jeffrey A. Greene; The Foundational Value Scale by Jason and Reichler.

Cognitive dimension of wisdom[148]

The cognitive dimension of wisdom refers to a person's ability to comprehend and understand life with its changing and sometimes conflicting domains. The various psychological assessment tools have produced the following cognitive attributes of a person considered to be 'wise'.

A wise person is considered having an extensive knowledge of the vicissitudes of life. This makes him or her tolerant of ambivalence and able to accept uncertainty in life.

Furthermore, a wise person is believed to comprehend the significance and deeper meaning of phenomena and events, particularly regarding intrapersonal and interpersonal matters. This knowledge includes his or her comprehension of the positive and negative aspects of human nature. In addition, a wise person is a good thinker, has a logical, rational mind and is intelligent. He or she comprehends the nature of human existence (e.g., mortality, vulnerability, emotionality).

As part of the cognitive dimension of wisdom, a wise person is observant and someone who knows that the importance of difficult life domains changes during the life span. Also, he or she knows that individual life goals and values may change during the life course and knows about conflicts between different life domains. Furthermore, someone who is considered wise knows about the interrelation of his/her individual existence with past, present, and future generations. This makes the wise person tolerant of ambiguity and uncertainty and able to make important decisions despite life's unpredictability and uncertainties. In addition, he or she is aware of, accepts and acts within one's own physical and intellectual limitations, and never stops learning to grow in knowledge. What is also mentioned is that a wise person is able and willing to understand a situation or phenomenon thoroughly. A wise person sees the essence of situations and sees things within larger context. He or she is perceptive and has a good problem-solving ability, offering solutions that are on the side of right and truth. Finally, a wise person can deal effectively in uncom-

---

[148] Ardelt, Monika. "Empirical Assessment of a Three-Dimensional Wisdom Scale" *Research on Aging,* Vol. 25 No. 3, May 2003, 275–324; Clayton, V.P., & Birren, J.E. 1980). "The development of wisdom across the life span: A re-examination of an ancient topic." In P.B. Baltes & O.G. Brim, Jr. (Eds.), *Life-span development and behavior* Vol. 3. (San Diego, CA: Academic Press, 1980). 103–135.

fortable (difficult to handle) interpersonal situations and expresses valuable insight into difficult life questions.

Reflective dimension of wisdom

The second dimension of wisdom identified by scientific research is *the reflective dimension*. This reflective dimension is considered a prerequisite for the development of the cognitive dimension that we have looked at. To understand life and perceive reality as it is, one needs to engage in reflective thinking. This includes looking at phenomena and events from many different perspectives and listening to all sides of an issue. This ability enables the wise person to avoid subjectivity and projections (i.e., to avoid blaming other people or circumstances for one's own situation or feelings). A wise person is someone who develops self-awareness and self-insight. He or she knows his or her strong and weak points, is not afraid to discuss errors in his or her life and tries to learn from his or her own mistakes. He or she also learns from experience and from other people's mistakes. Furthermore, a wise person is not afraid to change his or her mind because of this and is also open to consider advice given. Someone who is wise is thoughtful, introspective, and intuitive. A wise man or woman thinks carefully before speaking, acting, or making decisions. He or she can give sound judgment and good advice but knows when to give or withhold advice.

Affective dimension of wisdom

It is believed that a diminished self-centeredness and a better understanding of people's behavior are likely to improve one's affective emotions and demeanor toward others and tend to increase sympathetic and compassionate love. This then refers to the third dimension of wisdom that psychological research has identified, namely *the affective dimension.* This dimension refers to the presence of positive emotions and behavior toward other beings, such as feelings and acts of sympathy and compassion, and the absence of indifferent or negative emotions and behavior toward others. A wise person is caring and sensitive to others' feelings. He or she is concerned with helping others.

It is believed that in a person that is considered wise, these cognitive, reflective, and affective dimensions must be simultaneously present. Nevertheless, experts realize that they are seldom, if ever, fully, and always present in a person.

It is also a Weberian ideal type since only very few people might exist that would satisfy the above definition of a wise person. Although wisdom per se might be relatively difficult to find, it should still be possible to assess how close people come to this ideal state.[149]

Looking at characteristics of a wise person through the lens of philosophers and psychologists can be helpful and enlightening. Understanding wisdom as an integration of cognitive, reflective, and affective characteristics is useful, but not complete without a spiritual component. People who want to live their lives in submission to the Creator, with whom they have relationship of love and trust, recognize the value of the cognitive, reflective, and affective elements of wisdom, but they want to place these firmly on the foundation of the spiritual element. This is something that the researchers on wisdom cannot fathom:

> Past research also indicates that traditional religiosity and religious practices are unrelated to wisdom … This suggests that wisdom does not require religious faith but might benefit from a spirituality that is characterized by humility, gratitude, altruism, and compassionate love for others …[150]

The book of Proverbs strongly disagrees with this assessment when it gives its own characteristics of a wise person.

Six characteristics of a wise person in the book of Proverbs

When we read the book of Proverbs, we can identify the following six important characteristics of a wise person.

Godly

The fear of the LORD is the beginning of wisdom (9:10)

It has already been mentioned that from a biblical perspective a person cannot be considered wise without the core attitude of 'the fear of the LORD.' Such fear of the LORD is the foundation of wisdom, the starting point, the essence. We have seen earlier that 'the fear of the LORD' is a relational term, encompassing the totality of man's religious faith. It refers to one's commit-

---

149 Ardelt, Monika. "Empirical Assessment of a Three-Dimensional Wisdom Scale." *Research on Aging*, Vol. 25, No. 3, May 2003, 279.

150 Dilip V. Jeste, Monika Ardelt, Dan Blazer, Helena C. Kraemer, George Vaillant, and Thomas W. Meeks "Expert Consensus on Characteristics of Wisdom: A Delphi Method Study" *The Gerontologist* Vol. 50, No. 5, 668–680.

ment to God in faith, which includes obedience, loyalty, and love. If we desire to be a wise man or woman, it is vital that we cultivate the divine companionship through fearing the Lord.

> You have to be godly to be wise; and this is not because godliness pays, but because the only wisdom by which you can handle everyday things in conformity with their nature is the wisdom by which they were divinely made and ordered.[151]

Good

The proverbs of Solomon … for gaining wisdom … for receiving instruction in prudent behavior doing what is right and just and fair. (Proverbs 1:1–3)

In the wisdom the book of Proverbs upholds, the ethical aspect plays a prominent role:

> The whole of Proverbs is essentially about ethics, the distinction between good and evil is truly all pervasive. The book contains no technical advice on conducting any common activity be it agriculture, skilled work or trade. On the occasions where such daily activities are touched upon, the sages' concerns are confined to their ethical aspects.[152]

Throughout the book of Proverbs, the terms 'wisdom' and 'righteousness' are used interchangeably. One cannot be wise without being righteous. Other ethical terms that are used in close connection with wisdom are: justness, fairness, kindness, blameless, trustworthy.[153]

These characteristics fundamentally refer to someone's heart, but of course what is in the heart finds expression in specific acts. Throughout the book one finds descriptions of righteousness 'expressed in working clothes.'[154]

A wise person seeks the good of those around him[155] cares for the justice of the poor[156] and for the needs of their animals.[157] A wise person rejoices in jus-

---

[151] Kidner, 30.

[152] Frydrych, Thomas. *Living Under the Sun: Examination of Proverbs and Qoheleth.* (Boston: Brill, 2002), 176.

[153] See for example: Proverbs 2:7,9,20; 10:7,9,29; 13:6;19:1; 28:6; 11:5,20; 28:10.

[154] A term used by Kidner, page 33.

[155] 11:23,27.

[156] 29:7.

[157] 12:10.

tice[158] detests dishonesty[159] and hates what is false[160] and ill-gotten treasures.[161] A wise person seeks to live a blameless life;[162] he is generous with what he has.[163] The righteous are willing to disadvantage themselves to advantage the community.

> In the Holy Scriptures wisdom, when used of God and good men, always carries a strong moral connotation. It is conceived as being pure, loving, and good ... Wisdom, among other things, is the ability to devise perfect ends and to achieve those ends by the most perfect means. It sees the end from the beginning, so there can be no need to guess or conjecture. Wisdom sees everything in focus, each in proper relation to all, and is thus able to work toward predestined goals with flawless precision.[164]

Teachable

Whoever heeds life-giving correction will be at home among the wise. (Proverbs 15:31)[165]

An important characteristic that is given for a wise person in the book of Proverbs is that he or she is and remains teachable throughout his/her life. His willingness to learn will not diminish in old age. The conviction of a wise person is that one is never too old to learn.

The wise person is willing to make the appropriate adaptations necessary for lifelong learning. In such learning a wise person is open-minded and willing to seek insight from all disciplines, experiences, and cultures.

> A wise person is teachable, and this as much as any other single characteristic distinguishes the wise person from the fool. The wise person is open to instruction in all of its forms (teaching, correction, rebuke, dis-

---

[158] 21:15.

[159] 29:27.

[160] 13:15.

[161] 10:2.

[162] 20:7.

[163] 21:26.

[164] Tozer, A.W., *The Knowledge of the Holy* (San Francisco: Harper and Row, Publishers, 1961), 66.

[165] Other verses that express the same truth: Proverbs 1:8; 3:1; 9:9; 10:17; 13:1; 19:20.

cipline) and he learns from it, whereas the fool rejects it and continues to pursue his own self-destructive course.[166]

Even Solomon, although it is said of him that "he was wiser than anyone else" (1 Kings 4:31), incorporated in the wisdom material of Proverbs, material from Egyptian culture[167] and from foreigners like Agur and Lemuel.[168]

> Willingness to learn is characterized by a confidence in what knowledge a person has, the humility to believe that he or she simply cannot ever know everything, an openness to and interest in learning more, and a willingness to stumble in the pursuit of more knowledge.[169]

A wise person is not afraid to change his or her mind and is also open to consider advice given. He or she knows his or her strong and weak points, is not afraid to discuss errors in his or her life and tries to learn from his or her own mistakes. Someone who is wise is humble and open-minded. It takes humbleness to be willing to learn from people who are less mature. It takes humbleness to accept criticism and be willing to learn from it.

Someone who is wise is not wise in his own eyes,[170] she does not lean on her own understanding,[171] but he seeks knowledge,[172] she listens to instruction,[173] and advice,[174] because he acknowledges his limitations;[175] she accepts commands[176] and even welcomes reproof.[177] As a result he or she continues to grow in wisdom.[178] A wise person is a growing, maturing individual.

---

[166] Curtis and Brugaletta, 51.

[167] Proverbs 22:17–24:22.

[168] Proverbs 30:1; 31:1.

[169] Scott C. Brown. "Learning Across the Campus: How College Facilitates the Development of Wisdom." *Journal of College Student Development*, Volume 45, Number 2, March/April 2004, 134–148.

[170] Proverbs 3:7; 26:5,11,12,16.

[171] Proverbs 3:5.

[172] Proverbs 18:15.

[173] Proverbs 13:1.

[174] Proverbs 12:15.

[175] Proverbs 13:10.

[176] Proverbs 10:8.

[177] Proverbs 9:8; 12:1; 15:5; 17:10; 19:25; 21:11.

[178] Proverbs 1:5; Proverbs 9:9.

Knowledgeable

The wise store up knowledge (Proverbs 10:14)

Wisdom is often considered a kind of knowledge. Also, in the book of Proverbs wisdom is inseparable from knowledge, and wisdom is often used as a synonym for knowledge.[179]

> If knowledge is the accumulation of facts and intelligence the development of reason, wisdom is heavenly discernment. It is insight into the heart of things. Wisdom involves knowing God and the subtleties of the human heart. More than knowledge, it is the right application of knowledge in moral and spiritual matters, in handling dilemmas, in negotiating complex relationships.[180]

According to the book of Proverbs, the wise act with knowledge.[181] A wise person loves knowledge,[182] seeks it;[183] finds that it commends itself,[184] that it comes easily[185] and that knowledge is pleasing.[186] They experience that their knowledge protects them in temptation;[187] enables them to behave wisely and speak well[188] and increases their strength.[189]

It is important to realize that the knowledge that the book of Proverbs speaks of, is relational knowledge, which comes because of our fear of God. Without this, knowledge will lead us in the wrong direction. "To know the Deity is what knowledge means."[190]

> Nothing is further from the spirit of the sages than the idea of an autonomy of thinking, a humanism of the good life; in short of a wisdom

---

[179] Proverbs 2:6, 2:10,11; 14:6.

[180] Sanders, Oswald. *Spiritual Leadership.* (Chicago: Moody Press, 1994), 57.

[181] Proverbs 13:16; 14:18; 12:23; 15:2,7,14.

[182] 12:1.

[183] 15:14.

[184] 18:15.

[185] 8:9; 14:6.

[186] 2:10.

[187] 5:2.

[188] 12:23; 15:2,7; 17:27.

[189] 24:5. See Waltke I, 178.

[190] Moffat, quoted in Kidner, 78.

in the Stoic or Epicurean mode founded on the self-sufficiency of thought. This is why wisdom is held to be a gift of God in distinction to the "knowledge of good and evil" promoted by the Serpent.[191]

There are two specific kinds of knowledge that lie at the foundation of wisdom in the book of Proverbs:

Knowledge of the created order

> *By wisdom the Lord laid the earth's foundations,*
> *by understanding he sets the heavens in place,*
> *by His knowledge the watery depths were divided,*
> *and the clouds let drop the dew.*
> Proverbs 3:19,20

The book of Proverbs links wisdom with the created order. The verses above point out that the earth and heavens are made not by chance, but by God's wisdom.

> The point of this statement seems to be that wisdom is the principle that accounts for order and life found in creation."[192]

God is the sole Creator of the cosmos, and His wisdom provided the order of it. "Wisdom is concerned with discerning the order that the Lord has built into the creation."[193]

Knowledge of God's creation order provides us with a framework to order our lives. God ordered life in a certain way, building moral laws within its scheme. A wise person seeks to live within those constraints.[194] As God has created the cosmos according to His wise pattern, it is a characteristic of a wise person to live his/her life in discerning this pattern and order his/her life in acknowledgment of this.

---

[191] Paul Ricoeur, Essays on Biblical Interpretation, trans. Lewis Seymour Mudge (Philadelphia: Fortress, 1980), 88, quoted in Craig G. Bartholomew & Ryan P. O'Dowd, *Old Testament Wisdom Literature.*

[192] Waltke, Bruce. "The Book of Proverbs and Ancient Wisdom Literature," *Bibliotheca Sacra* 136 (1979), 233.

[193] Bartholomew, Craig G., and Ryan P. O'Dowd. *Old Testament Wisdom Literature: A Theological Introduction.* (Downers Grove, Ill.: IVP Academic, 2011), 74.

[194] Bland, Dave. *Proverbs and the Formation of Character.* (Eugene, Oregon: Cascade Books, 2015), 3.

> If the Lord with wisdom as his tool accomplished the wonders of the various phases of creation – setting the earth on its foundations by splitting the primeval waters and setting the heavens in their appointed place and watering the earth with dew from its clouds – think, what his revealed wisdom will do in the lives of those who find it.[195]

But one cannot access God's order for creation independently of the fear of the Lord.

> Wisdom is concerned with life lived according to the grain of creation … and seeking to draw our lives into harmony with the created order. The key to such wise and harmonious living is the fear of the Lord – faith in and obedience to Yahweh preconditions our access to God's cosmic designs. … Grounded in the fear of the Lord, wisdom looks to the creation and finds the patterns that are meant to give order to our moral, social, economic and political living … It is only as we are deeply rooted in the Lord and instructed by him that we are able to read the creation order correctly.[196]

Knowledge of the deed-destiny nexus

"The righteous person is rescued from trouble, and it falls on the wicked instead." (Proverbs 11:8)

Intricately linked to the knowledge of the created order[197] is the knowledge of what is called the 'deed-destiny' nexus, also referred to as 'deed-outcome' nexus, or 'character-destiny' nexus, or 'deed-consequence' nexus. The above verse is an illustration of this, one of the many that we find in the book of Proverbs.

> Proverbs presents a "world order" involving "deed and destiny" that is to say," What you do now will determine what will happen then." A more precise formulation is a *character -› conduct -› consequence connection – that is, what you are determines what you will become.[198]*

A characteristic of a wise person is the knowledge of this deed-destiny connection and more specifically the relationship of the Lord to this nexus. The

---

[195] Waltke, 261.

[196] Bartholomew, 91, 96, 97, 291.

[197] In fact, some would say that this is what is meant by the creation order.

[198] Waltke I, 73.

wise person knows that this deed-destiny, or cause-consequence nexus is not an impersonal order, but a personal divine retribution, although the method of this process is not clearly spelled out. He maintains a balance between *human freedom* to plan carefully, to choose the right path to succeed and prosper, and take responsibility for their own destiny, and *divine sovereignty*, realizing that God is in total control of human affairs and determines their outcome.

> While it is true that the sages developed plans and strategies by which to live, they did not believe in a created order that operated mechanically. The sages do attempt to establish order to life. They have an interest in discovering certain predictable patterns of experiences. Even given this interest, the order which they discover underlying the experiences of life are not fate producing. They did not themselves as the captains in creating their own destiny. The sage does not wrestle with the concept of a rigid order as much as with the person of God. A dialectic exists between the predictable order of creation and the free work of God. Wisdom sought not to master life but to navigate it.[199]

This connection between deed and destiny, seems to be best described as 'character-consequence', because often the proverbs that speak on this do not concern individual acts and their consequences, but refer to repeated behavior.

It is the long-term character and direction of a person or group (as 'righteous' or 'wicked') which determines life consequences and 'destiny'.[200]

Another thing to keep in mind regarding the 'character-destiny' nexus is that the book of Proverbs also includes sayings that contradict this character-consequence concept. This particularly is found in the 'better-than' sayings, such as "Better a little with the fear of the Lord than great wealth with turmoil. Better a small serving of vegetables with love than a fattened calf with hatred." (Proverbs 15:16,17)

> There are situations in which the character-consequence theme is fitting, and there are situations in which the better-than proverbs are more appropriate. The wise person will know which is which.[201]

---

[199] Bland, 151.

[200] Van Leeuwen, quoted in Bartholomew, OT Wisdom Literature, 271, 272.

[201] Bartholomew, 273.

Emotionally Intelligent[202]

A wise person is an emotionally intelligent person. He or she has good social skills. A wise person says and does the right thing at the right time. They express the appropriate emotions at the right time. They exercise self-control and use and express their emotions appropriately.

> Wisdom is similar to what today we often call emotional intelligence. … Proverbs is a book that on the practical level offers to make its attentive reader wise (emotionally intelligent).[203]

We can identify the five main elements of emotional intelligence: Self-Awareness; Self-Regulation; Motivation; Empathy; Social Skills,[204] as characteristics of a wise person in the book of Proverbs.

Self-awareness

The wisdom of the prudent is to give thought to their ways … (Proverbs 14:8)[205]

One of the keystones of emotional intelligence is self-awareness. In the EQ theory this is particularly focused on recognizing and understanding our emotions and the effect they have on others. Biblical wisdom expands this self-awareness to a broader level, including knowing our awareness of God and our role in creation and our dependability and accountability toward our Creator. In fact, it is one of the stated purposes of the book of Proverbs to provide insight, understanding, discernment.[206] A wise person gives time to a moral reflection on his conduct. Someone who is wise can assess and analyze his own emotions and behavior and realize where it leads. This helps him to think before acting or speaking. A wise person understands his emotions and the effect these have on others.

A wise person is also aware of his own strengths and weaknesses, which is reflected in his prayer to God for help and guidance.[207]

---

[202] The term 'Emotional Intelligence' was created by two researchers, Peter Salovey and John Mayer in 1989, and popularized by Daniel Goleman in 1995 in his book *Emotional Intelligence.* (New York: BantamBooks, 1995).

[203] Tremper Longman III, *The Fear of the Lord is Wisdom*, 7,9.

[204] According to Goleman in his book Emotional Intelligence.

[205] Other verses that express a similar truth are Proverbs 14:12,15,16; 21:29.

[206] Proverbs 1:2; 4:1.

[207] For example, Agur in Proverbs 30:7–9.

Self-regulation

Fools give full vent to their rage, but the wise bring calm in the end. (Proverbs 29:11)

A second key element of Emotional Intelligence is 'self-regulation', referring to managing one's emotions and impulses, controlling them, and not be controlled by them. Once we understand ourselves, we are better able to control ourselves.

The ability to control our emotions and impulses and express them at the right time and to the appropriate degree is an important aspect of wisdom. Someone who is wise can control his or her emotions and impulses, be it anger, lust, speech, greed, envy, sleep, appetite, or thoughts.[208]

With its apt saying "Like a city whose walls are broken through is a person who lacks self-control." (25:28) the book of Proverbs gives a great analogy.

> The external defense of a walled city is compared to the internal defense of self-control that human possess. Lack of self-restraint leaves one vulnerable to emotions and desires that wage war within. Self-control enables a person to hold those desires in check and channel them for productive use … The person who controls the self accomplishes more than the one who controls others.[209]

Self-Motivation

Better a little with the fear of the Lord than great wealth with turmoil. (Proverbs 15:16)

Knowing ourselves and controlling ourselves enables us to use our emotions and this leads to the third aspect of Emotional Intelligence: self-motivation. In the understanding of EQ this refers to our motivation in life, to achieve, to pursue our goals with persistency, our reasons for doing something, and being clear about what we want to achieve.

The motive for living a life that is considered wise is not health, wealth, or prosperity. Although the book of Proverbs does state many times that wise behavior will make live better and richer, both personally, as well as corpo-

---

[208] See Proverbs 10:19; 13:16; 14:29; 15:18; 16:32; 17:27; 18:13,17; 19:11; 20:13,25; 21:17; 23:20–21; 23:26–28; 24:30–34; 25:28; 29:3.

[209] Bland, 47.

rately, the motive that drives wise behavior is the fear of the Lord. A wise person is resolved to not allow secondary goals to distract him/her from the more important goals. Wise people understand that wisdom is better than strength and wealth; that the fear of the Lord, good relationships with people, righteousness, humility, integrity are all better than wealth; that loneliness is better than a stormy marriage relationship; that reality is better than appearance; that modesty is better than shame; that a close neighbor is better than a far relative; that an open rebuke is better than hidden love; that control of self is better than control of others; that what is right is better than what is successful.[210]

Empathy

Let love and faithfulness never leave you, bind them around your neck, write them on the tablet of your heart. (3:3)

The righteous care for the needs of their animals, but the kindest acts of the wicked are cruel (Proverbs 12:10)

Once we have a good understanding and control of our emotions, we can grow into our ability to understand the emotions of others. This is empathy, the fourth element of EQ, which is recognizing and understanding another person's feelings, or at least their emotional reactions to things. Empathy is closely related to compassion which is one of the key characteristics of a wise person.

A wise person, who is also called a righteous person in the book of Proverbs, is encouraged to act in love and faithfulness towards others. He is sensitive to the needs of others, even to the needs of animals (Proverbs 12:10), which shows compassion has become part of their way of life.

> The proverb probably entails an argument *a minores ad maiores*, if one shows mercy in the lesser creation, how much more in the greater.[211]

It is because of their respect for, their fear of, their Creator that wise people empathize with others, be it the needy and the poor or even their enemies, who are also valued by the same Creator.[212]

---

[210] Proverbs 3:14; 8:11,19; 12:9; 15:16,17; 16:8,16,19,32; 17:1; 19:1,22; 21:9,19; 22:1; 25:7,24; 27:5,10; 28:6.

[211] Waltke, I, 526.

[212] Proverbs 11:16,17; 14:21,31;17:5; 21:13; 24:17,18; 29:7.

Social Skill

The words of the reckless pierce like swords, but the tongue of the wise brings healing. (Proverbs 12:18)

A king's wrath is a messenger of death, but the wise will appease it. (Proverbs 16:14)

The final aspect that is given of Emotional Intelligence, is social skills, which refers to the ability to influence the feelings of others. Cole describes social skills as "friendliness with a purpose." The purpose could be personal, organizational, or societal benefit. This ability refers to handling relationships in a satisfactory manner and relates to interpersonal communication and dealing with conflict.

An important characteristic of a wise person, as described in the book of Proverbs is that he is a peacebuilder, an encourager, one who can bring healing and reconciliation and peace among people. He provides vitality in a community. He or she is someone who can be trusted. His words are gentle and kind. She builds trust.[213]

Having seen that wise people are emotionally intelligent, this does not automatically mean that people who score high on EQ are wise people, because without the fear of the Lord there is no wisdom in the Biblical sense of the word.

Humble

Humility is the fear of the Lord ... (Proverbs 22:4a)

Wisdom's instruction is to fear the Lord, and humility comes before honor. (Proverbs 15:33)

When pride comes, then comes disgrace, but with humility comes wisdom. (Proverbs 11:2)

We have already seen that humility is a key characteristic of someone who fear God, which is of someone who is wise. A wise person lives in daily submission to God and accepts his subordinate position before God.

We can recognize someone that is humble in his or her willingness to be open to correction, to learn from others. Someone who is humble will not easily fall

---

[213] Proverbs 11:29,30; 13:14; 14:35; 15:4.

into the temptation of hardening one's heart before God or men.[214] A wise person considers humility more important than being wealthy,[215] and better than pretension.[216] A wise person is modest[217] and not afraid to acknowledge his ignorance;[218] he doesn't boast about tomorrow, because he doesn't know what a day may bring;[219] he abstains from self-praise and self-promotion,[220] understanding that the way to honor is through humility.[221]

A wise person who is humble has an accurate view of who God is and has an accurate view of what his place is in the world that God created. Because of this they can submit to God, appreciate other and value themselves in an appropriate way.

Questions for further reflection

1. Which of the characteristics of a wise person given in the book of Proverbs is the most valuable to you? Explain.

2. Which one(s) are the best developed in your life and which one(s) are the least developed?

3. An aspect of the reflective dimension of wisdom mentioned in this chapter is that a wise person can look at phenomena and events from many different perspectives and listening to all sides of an issue. How do you aim to do this?

----

[214] Proverbs 28:14.

[215] Proverbs 16:19.

[216] Proverbs 12:19.

[217] Proverbs 18:12.

[218] Proverbs 30:2–4.

[219] Proverbs 27:1.

[220] Proverbs 27:2; 25:6,7.

[221] Proverbs 18:12; 29:23.

CHAPTER 6
THE WISE MAN AND HIS DILIGENCE

Earlier in this book we have compared our quest for wisdom with digging for gold, which requires preparation, determination, and perseverance. We can call it diligence.

It is impossible to become a wise person without diligence. We have already seen that having wisdom coming into our heart is not just a gift from God that He put into us, while we are asleep. Wisdom will be given to those who are determined to get it, with zeal, eagerly, persistently, wholeheartedly, as determined as a gold-digger is to find a piece of gold. Diligence is the prerequisite for becoming wise. We hear Woman Wisdom say: *"I love those who love me; And those who diligently seek me will find me." (Proverbs 8:17)*

Diligence is one of the characteristics of God and therefore, it should become part of those whose aim is to fear God in all they do.

In this chapter we will reflect on diligence in the context of wisdom. The book of Proverbs considers diligence one of the key characteristics of a wise person. It is also intricately linked to other characteristics. We have already seen that that a wise person is an emotionally intelligent person, who is always able to self-regulate himself and keep his or her emotions and impulses under control. In fact, this is a necessary first step for diligence. Without self-control it is impossible to be diligent.

> Diligence moves a person to move quickly to accept stretching challenges, to stay focused on what is crucial in the long run rather than living for what is convenient at the present and to grasp decisively the opportunities that God presents.[222]

In the book of Proverbs there are three Hebrew terms used to for diligence. The word 'mahir' refers to quickness, promptness, and readiness. A diligent person moves quickly to accept a challenge or engage in a mission. Another Hebrew term that is used for diligence, 'sahar' refers to seeking something earnestly and wholeheartedly, despite difficulty and to maintain a clear focus.

---

[222] Estes, 236.

The third term that is used for diligence is 'harus' and this expression refers to what is sharp, decisive, planning one's steps carefully.

We will investigate this in more detail now.

Diligence is necessary for growing into wisdom

… let the wise listen and add to their learning. (1:5)

Our quest for wisdom is a life-long process. Although, as we have already seen, growing old does not automatically mean that we become wiser, we should grow in wisdom as we mature in age. But this requires challenging work and perseverance on our part. An important aspect of growing in wisdom as we grow older is to maintain a learning posture as long as we live.

One of the characteristics of a wise person is that he or she realizes he needs to continue to grow in wisdom. To become wiser still. One of the stated purposes of the book of Proverbs is that the wise 'add to their learning' (1:5). Once we have tasted the richness of wisdom, we want to have it increasingly. This requires diligence. Once wisdom begins to manifest itself in us, it is growth will also be result of continuing diligence. As we have seen this means, among other things, to learn from life by regarding, reflecting, responding, and remembering. Eugene Peters points out that growth occurs because of long obedience in the same direction.[223]

The motive for diligence is the fear of the LORD

… always be zealous for the fear of the Lord. (23:17)

As we have seen repeatedly, the attitude of fearing God is essential for becoming wise and for growing in wisdom. The fear of the LORD is also the main driving force, the motive for our diligence. Although the book of Proverbs speaks a lot about the results of diligence and the consequences of a lack of it, it is not health, wealth and success that needs to stimulate our diligence. These are by-products of something else, namely the fear of God, the Knowing of the Holy One, the intimate relationship of trust of and obedience to the sole Creator of heaven and earth, Who Alone is worthy of our deepest devotion.

---

[223] Peterson, Eugene H. *A Long Obedience in the Same Direction* (Downers Grove, Ill: InterVarsity, 1980).

Although Proverbs repeats time and again that diligence will be rewarded, the chief motivation for diligence is not personal prosperity, but the fear of the Lord. We are diligent because the Lord has given us life and its specific tasks and roles. Our awe of him motivates us to be diligent in how we carry these out.[224]

It is because of this that a wise person seeks to be diligent, not only in pursuing and growing into wisdom, but also in maintaining the relationship with the Most High (Proverbs 8:17,34). We need to be diligent in maintaining a vibrant and growing relationship with Him, by consistently walking in His ways and listening to His word.

In the book of Proverbs, diligence not only refers to our work,[225] but diligence is also applied to parenting.[226] A parent disciplines his children diligently, that is in an intentional, decisive way.

Diligence is a heart issue

Keep thy heart with all diligence (4:23)

The 'heart' in the Bible does not refer to the muscle that pumps the blood through our veins, but the term refers to our inner being, our core personality. It involves our mind, emotions, and will. It is the control center of our life, the spring from where everything else flows, particularly our thoughts, our words, and our decisions. No wonder we are admonished to keep it, to treasure it, to guard it, to preserve it with all diligence. If we are diligent in taking care of the inner man, it will have enormous implications for all other aspects of our life.

Keeping our heart with all diligence means paying sufficient attention to the inner man, and not be too occupied with the outer being.

> If my private world is in order, it will be because I have determined that every day will before me a day of growth in knowledge and wisdom.[227]

---

[224] Source unknown.

[225] "Poor is he who works with a negligent hand, but the hand of the diligent makes rich. He who gathers in summer is a son who acts wisely, but he who sleeps in harvest is a son who acts shamefully." (Proverbs 10:4,5)

[226] Proverbs 13:24.

[227] MacDonald, Gordon. *Ordering your Private World*, (Nashville: Thomas Nelson Publishers, 1985), 105.

Diligence begins in the heart, before it becomes visible in our way of life. Not many people are lazy, or passive in all areas of their lives. Sometimes someone's passion comes alive for sports, or injustice, or environmental issues, while in other areas of life he or she could not care less. Diligence shows what we value most.

Diligence leads to skillfulness

Diligent hands will rule, but laziness ends in slave labor. (12:24)

Do you see people who do their work with diligence? They will serve before kings; they will not serve before the obscure. (22:29)

As we have seen the Hebrew word used for wisdom *'hokmah'* often refers to a skill, an expertise. In his book *Outlier: The Story of Success*, Malcolm Gladwell describes his research among the abilities of top performers (e.g. chess players, composers, musicians, mathematicians). Based on this he argues that to achieve true expertise in any skill is a matter of practicing, albeit in the correct way, for at least ten thousand hours.[228] Ten thousand hours works out to be around twenty hours per week for ten years. If we want to see wisdom and its characteristics grow in our lives, we cannot settle for a quick fix. We need persistence, endurance, and determinism.

The diligence of a wise person makes him excel in what he does.

The diligence of the wise enables him to lead a focused, intentional life

He who works his land will have abundant food, but the one who chases fantasies will have his fill of poverty. (28:19)

A discerning man keeps wisdom in view, but a fool's eyes wander to the ends of the earth. (17:24)

The heart of the discerning acquires knowledge; the ears of the wise seek it out. (18:15)

The opposite if living diligently is chasing fantasies, or pursuing one dream after another, whatever is fashionable at that moment. Some people spend their lives thinking about unattainable goals, based on unrealistic expecta-

---

[228] Outliers, Gladwell M. *The Story of Success*. (San Francisco: Little, Brown and Company, 2008).

tions. Others might begin on a course of action with enthusiasm but get distracted when other more interesting things come along. Their life is a string of unfinished plans and projects. Some people are continually taken in by the immediate, the urgent, and as a result hey have no time or attention for what is important in the long run.

The diligence of the wise person helps her to focus on what is important eventually.[229]

A wise person does not chase fantasies but lives intentionally. Diligence means giving hundred percent, giving our absolute best. Diligence shows where we put our effort in. Diligence is being fully engaged and persevering.

> The root of the term translated "diligence" has a number of different connotations. The most literal connotation is to "cut or sharpen" something. Metaphorically the term is used of sharpness as an attitude – being decisive and intentional. If you are "diligent" you act in a decisive, intentional way.[230]

When we realize that we are created by a good and loving God, who does not waste anything and does everything with a purpose, our intention should be to seek His will for our lives in accordance with whom He made us to be. Author Dr. Robert J. Clinton defines a focused life as follows:

> A life dedicated to exclusively carrying out God's effective purpose through it, by identifying the focus issues, that is: a) the life purpose, b) effective methodology, c) major role, and d) ultimate contribution which allows an increasing prioritization of life's activities around the focal issues, and results in a satisfying life of being and doing.[231]

The diligence of a wise person maintains in him or her a sense of urgency.

Diligence rightly understood is urgency under control.[232]

---

229 Proverbs 11:27.

230 Stephen A. Ratliff; In his sermon "A Life of Diligence", on June 21, 2009. https://static1.squarespace.com/static/5c40e5604611a0abbac80cf4/t/5d274fa6bfc6ea0001b1e045/1562857382617/2009_07_19_Sermon.pdf.

231 Clinton, Robert J. *Strategic Concepts that Clarify a Focused Life*. (Altadena, CA: Barnabas Publishers, 2005),1.

232 Curtis and Brugaletta, 101.

The diligence of the wise helps her to plan ahead

The plans of the diligent lead to profit, as surely as haste leads to poverty. (21:5)

A wise person is someone who live his or her life with a continuous awareness of, and commitment to, fearing God, which involves living in agreement with God's order, obeying His will and accepting His authority in all aspects of life. God is a God of plans. He has plans, good plans, for the universe, and for all His creatures, including you and me. His plans are for His glory and the well-being of everything he made. He will make sure that His plans will be accomplished in His time and His way. Knowing this, should not make us fatalistic, or passive. On the contrary: knowing God has good plans for us and has created us for a purpose should encourage us to seek to live purposeful lives and be serious in taking responsibility for our own lives. This includes planning.

> We should assume that the diligent creatively plan within the framework of God's revealed will and by nature act accordingly, but, marking the antithesis, the one who hastens to get rich acts without the reckoning with the divine order.[233]

A wise, diligent person knows the importance of planning. He is thoughtful, not hasty.

> Elsewhere the diligent person stands over against the lethargic sluggard (10:4; 12:24,27, 13:4), but here he stands opposed to the rash and imprudent. The lazy are defective in action; the hasty, in thought. The prudence of the diligent now consists in his wise planning in contrast to ill-conceived and misdirected actions (cf 11:24–28). Rashi rightly defined the diligent as "a righteous man who goes in truth and with clear-cut judgment … Contrary to the expectations of those who do what is right in their own eyes (see 21:2) the restrained diligent surprisingly gain only more than they invested (cf. Romans 2:7; Hebrews 6:12) and the unrestrained hasty person loses only what is essential to life."[234]

A wise person knows that zeal without knowledge is not good and that by being hasty he can miss the way.[235] We are encouraged to learn such diligent, wise planning from ants:

---

[233] Waltke, II, 172.

[234] Waltke, II, 172.

[235] Proverbs 19:2 "It is not good to have zeal without knowledge, nor to be hasty and miss the way."

Go to the ant, you sluggard; consider its ways and be wise … it stores it provisions in summer and gathers its food at harvest … (Proverbs 6:6–8)

Ants are creatures of little strength, yet they store their food in the summer. (Proverbs 30:25)

> … The ant's ways … essentially teach self-discipline, foresight, and industry – more specifically prudent industry … God provides food … but the ant must diligently harvest it in the right way at the right time …[236]

Wise planning involves careful preparation and seizing the right opportunities and not neglect the possibilities.[237] A wise person is alert, attentive and ready.[238]

… staying awake is a hallmark of diligence.[239]

The diligence of the wise helps him to prioritize

In his desire to encourage his readers/listeners to be serious in their quest for wisdom Solomon has included seventeen so-called 'better-than' proverbs in the book. In these proverbs two things are compared and assigned a relative value. A wise person has learned to prioritize his or her life around those characteristics, circumstances, attitudes that are best, in comparison to their alternatives.

1. Better to be a nobody and yet have a servant than pretend to be somebody and have no food. (12:9)

2. Better a little with the fear of the Lord, tan great wealth with turmoil. (15:16)

3. Better a meal of vegetables where there is love, than a fattened calf with hatred. (15:17)

---

[236] Waltke, I, 336–338.

[237] 10:4,5 Lazy hands make for poverty, but diligent hands bring wealth. He who gathers crops in summer is a prudent son, but he who sleeps during harvest is a disgraceful son.

[238] Proverbs 20:13 Do not love sleep or you will grow poor, stay awake and you will have food to spare. "The practical lesson is that one should diligently attend to wisdom and observe the word carefully. To fail to do so is folly, for the fool does not know how to see or hear properly (17:24; 23:9)" (Fox, 668).

[239] Anders, 28.

4. Better a little with righteousness, than much gain with injustice. (16:8)

5. How much better to get wisdom than gold, to choose understanding rather than silver. (16:16)

6. Better to be lowly in spirit and among the oppressed than to share plunder with the proud. (16:19)

7. Better a patient person than a warrior, one with self-control than one who takes a city. (16;32)

8. Better a dry crust with peace and quiet than a house full of feasting with strife. (17:1)

9. Better a poor man whose walk is blameless than a fool whose lips are perverse. (19:1)

10. ... better to be poor than a liar (19:22)

11. Better to live on a corner of the roof than share a house with a quarrelsome wife (21:9) (25:24)

12. Better to live in a desert, than with a quarrelsome and ill-tempered wife. (21:19)

13. A good name is more desirable than great riches, to be esteemed is better than silver or gold. (22:1)

14. It is better for him to say to you, "Come up here," than for him to humiliate you before his nobles. (25:7)

15. Better is open rebuke than hidden love (27:5)

16. better a neighbor nearby than a relative far away. (27:10)

17. Better a poor man whose walk is blameless than a rich man whose ways are perverse. (28:6)

These seventeen are examples that might be multiplied in our lives with many more. It requires wisdom to distinguish wise behavior from foolish behavior, wise responses from foolish responses, wise choices from foolish choices. It requires diligence to consistently choose the best over the good and to hold on to what is good.[240]

---

[240] "Hold on to instruction, do not let it go, guard it well, for it is your life." (Proverbs 4:13)

Diligence makes the wise allergic to laziness

I went past the field of a sluggard, past the vineyard of the man who lacks judgment; thorns had come up everywhere, the ground was covered with weeds, and the stone wall was in ruins. I applied my heart to what I observed and learned a lesson from what I saw … (24:30,31)

One of the characteristics of a wise person is that he or she is a keen observer of life and learns from what he sees. One of the people that Solomon draws our attention to in the book of Proverbs is a sluggard, a lazy person.

Diligent behavior frequently is contrasted in with the ineffective approach of the sluggard. The picture that the book of Proverbs paints of a sluggard helps us to understand why a wise and diligent person is allergic to this kind of life-style.

A sluggard is reluctant to begin on a project. He postpones his or her tasks if possible. He asks for a little respite repeatedly.[241] He lets opportunities slip away.[242] Not only is a sluggard slow in beginning things, he or she finds its equally hard to finish what he started. Solomon humorously expresses this: "The sluggard buries his hand in the dish, he will not even bring it back to his mouth." (29:4; 26:15)[243]

Also, a sluggard continually finds excuses to rationalize his behavior. Some of these excuses seem to be ridiculous. For example, "The sluggard says, "There is a lion outside!" or "I will be murdered in the streets!"" (22:13).

Sometimes a sluggard is contrasted with someone who is upright,[244] which seems to indicate that he is not only lazy but also immoral, making up things that are not there, distorting the truth, lying.

Of course, such behavior is considered foolish, but it is hard convincing the sluggard of this, because we also read that "the sluggard is wiser in his own eyes, than seven men who answer discreetly." (26:16)

---

[241] Proverbs 6:9–11; 24:33,34.

[242] Proverbs 20:4 "A sluggard does not plough in season, so at harvest time he looks but finds nothing."

[243] See also Proverbs 12:27 "The lazy man does not roast his game, but the diligent man prizes his possessions."

[244] Proverbs 15:19.

The consequences of a sluggard's lifestyle are clearly spelled out. He is restless, because his desires are not satisfied,[245] helpless[246] and useless, causing damage and irritation[247] to those who want to make use of him.

A diligent person is often put in sharp contrast with the sluggard. Whereas a sluggard's lifestyle easily leads to scarcity and poverty, that of a diligent person brings wealth.[248] Whereas through laziness someone misses good opportunities to grow and flourish, the diligent seizes the times and blossoms.[249] While a lazy person can get carried away with fantasies and empty talk, the diligent person perseveres in the tasks at hand and profits.[250] Whereas through laziness people often get stuck in the mud, the diligent keep growing and improve their skills.[251] Whereas the drowsiness of the lazy can lead to frustration, the zeal of the diligent bears fruit.[252] Whereas the lazy person sees obstacles, the diligent sees opportunities.[253] Whereas a lazy person neglects to maintain what he has and thereby brings it to ruins, the diligent man values his possessions enough to care for them and takes full advantage of what he has gained.[254] Whereas a lazy person continually craves for a little more for himself, the diligent has abundance which they are willing to share.[255] Where-

---

[245] Proverbs 13:4; 21:25,26.

[246] Proverbs 15:19.

[247] Proverbs 10:26; 18:9.

[248] Proverbs 10:4,5; 19:15. "Although the lazy/diligent proverbs offer a promise of wellbeing through images of material wealth and lack … these promises ought not to be understood only as literal promises of literal wealth … They function to persuade the hearer of the value and desirability of a variety of virtues (working the land toiling, remaining active) and the undesirability of certain vices (pursuing vanity, idle talk, love of sleep, slackness, lack of sense)." (Sandoval, the discourse of wealth and poverty, 138).

[249] Proverbs 10:4,5; 20:4.

[250] Proverbs 12:11; 14:23; 28:19.

[251] Proverbs 12:24. "To put it bluntly, the diligent rise to the top and the lazy sink to the bottom." (Ross, Proverbs, p. 973) (Waltke, I, 541).

[252] Proverbs 13:4; 21:25,26. Proverbs 13:4 assumes that everything needful for life is richly available under God's good hand, but it is non-existent for the sluggard." (Waltke, I, 555).

[253] Proverbs 15:19.

[254] Proverbs 24:30–34; 27:23–27.

[255] Proverbs 21:25,26.

as a lazy man loses focus and lacks follow-through, a diligent man is decisive and intentional.[256]

> We are diligent because we want to align our lives with God and His ways. We are diligent because we don't want to waste our lives and all the opportunities that God gives us. We are diligent because life is too short to fritter it away. A diligent person is wholehearted in whatever he does. Instead of being tentative or passive or luke-warm, a diligent person has a sense of what s/he should be doing and therefore "goes for it." Another way to talk about it is to say that the diligent person is "passionate" about life. If you're diligent, you live "like you mean it." (Stephen A. Ratliff)

A diligent woman

The last words of the book of Proverbs contain an acrostic poem,[257] about an excellent woman. This woman encompasses many of the traits of wisdom that have been discussed in this book. She is a woman who fears God (vs 30), is trustworthy (vs 11) is kind to the poor and needy (vs 20), she speaks with wisdom (vs 26). She is also diligent and energetic. We read about her that "She watches over the affairs of her household and does not eat the bread of idleness." (31:27)

> The Valiant Woman is diligent. Proverbs portrays her diligence in three ways: 1) Hard work; 2) Long-term planning; 3) Profitability. As result of her diligence in these ways, she is confident about the future.[258]

Women and man who want to be wise need diligence, not only in their pursuit of wisdom and in their desire to fear God, but in many other areas of life, such as dealing with money, the use of the tongue, relating to friends and one's spouse and developing a lifestyle that please God. We will look at these topics in the next chapters of this book.

---

[256] Proverbs 12:27.

[257] acrostic means: the initial consonant of each verse follow the order of the Hebrew alphabet.

[258] Waltke, Bruce and Alice Matthews "The wise worker is diligent" in the *Theology of Work project,* www.theologyofwork.org.

Questions for further reflection

1. In what areas of life do you need to grow in diligence?

2. What do you think is the best way to be cured from laziness?

3. The book of Proverbs encourages us to look at ants to learn diligence. Can you think of other examples in nature that can inspire us towards diligence?

CHAPTER 7
THE WISE MAN AND HIS MONEY

Honor the Lord with your wealth … (Proverbs 3:9)

The way a person deals with money and materialism says a lot about his or her character. Money has been a great blessing to many people, allowing them to do good to society. But money has also been a great curse, destroying people's lives and breaking up families. Often money is a power that controls us rather than something that we can control. Jesus spoke of money as an idol, a god, mammon. Money can become an idol that demands our loyalty, our commitment our worship and that provides joy, pleasure, material goods and many more things in return. When money becomes an idol, another god, it can compete with our commitment and loyalty towards the Sovereign Creator of heaven and earth. No wonder, Jesus said that one cannot serve God and Mammon. One must choose between one and the other. This same sentiment we can find in the book of Proverbs. We have already learned that a wise person is someone who fears the Lord, who gives His utmost loyalty to God, who puts weight on His commandments, His Word, and His will. Such a commitment undoubtedly has consequences for once's relationship with money.

The book of Proverbs has a lot to say about wealth and poverty, rich and poor.

> The book of Proverbs is an ideal text in which to consider the discourse of wealth and poverty for it draws on wealth and poverty language more than any other book in the Hebrew Bible.[259]

The book of Proverbs does not condemn being rich, but it has a lot to say about its snares. We learn from the book two important lessons, namely that a wise person knows the proper value of wealth and that a wise person honors God with his wealth.

A wise person knows the proper value of wealth

A wise person understands the proper value of wealth and realizes that it does not define who he is, because his significance as a human being is not valued

---

[259] Sandoval, Timothy J., *The Discourse of Wealth and Poverty in the Book of Proverbs.* (Leiden: Brill, 2006), 5.

by money.[260] A wise person perceives that he can do much good with his wealth, but that it can also attract the wrong kinds of friends.[261]

A wise person believes that money is not the most valuable commodity in life, and that pursuing material wealth should not be one's focus in life. Wisdom gives us proper restraint in the pursuit of money,[262] avoiding the temptation to spend it on pleasure[263] and gluttony.[264] Wealth can easily distort our perspectives of what is truly valuable and important in life.

A wise person has come to see that there are at least six things that are of more value in life than material wealth.

Wisdom is more valuable than wealth

For she (Wisdom) is more profitable than silver and yields better returns than gold. She is more precious than rubies; nothing you desire can compare with her. (Proverbs 3:14,15)

My (Wisdom) fruit is better than fine gold; what I yield surpasses choice silver. (Proverbs 8:19)

How much better to get wisdom than gold, to get insight rather than silver. (Proverbs 16:16)

The book you are reading is about our quest for wisdom. In our pursuit for wisdom, in our desire to grow in wisdom and becoming a wise person, we learn from the book of Proverbs that what we are looking for is of the utmost value. If we want to grow in wisdom, we must put this desire on top of all other desires, particularly our desire for wealth. Our pursuit of wealth can hinder our pursuit of wisdom. It is not until we see that wisdom is more profitable than gold or silver, or the modern equivalent such as house, car, goods, holidays, luxury, that we will seek wisdom with all our heart. We must really want it, to get it and to have it become part of our lives. Of course, as we will see wisdom and wealth can go together, but only in this order. Wealth without

---

[260] "Rich and poor have this in common: The Lord is the Maker of them all." (Proverbs 22:2).

[261] See Proverbs 14:20; 19:4,6.

[262] Proverbs 23:4.

[263] Proverbs 21:17.

[264] Proverbs 23:20,21.

wisdom makes us fools in the eyes of God. Wealth without wisdom may be vulgarity or greed or ruthless individualism.[265]

A good name preferable to wealth

A good name is more desirable than great riches; to be esteemed is better than silver or gold. (Proverbs 22:1)

A wise person not only knows that wisdom is more valuable than wealth, but also that having a good name is of higher value than wealth. A good name refers to one's reputation, to someone's character and can also refer to how someone is remembered. A good name builds trust and confidence. It might be hard to ever overcome reputational damage. Towards the end of his live Solomon himself violated this principle.

> Solomon rightly chose wisdom and with it came a good name and loving favor. When wisdom failed him in his religious compromises and his oppressive use of power, not even the immense riches could salvage his name.[266]

A good name is valuable. It builds confidence, it provides power, it opens doors. It is something to treasure. A good name is not just an external matter. A good name reflects a good character. A good name refers to someone with integrity and authenticity. The saying is particularly relevant in an honor/shame culture, where one's name refers to one's personal identity as it is recognized and respected in the community. Someone with a good name is accepted and esteemed. We cannot choose a good name. It is something that is given to us by others because of what they see in our lives and conduct. Of course, we can choose to do everything in our power to maintain this good name. Many people lose their good name by the abuse of wealth or trying to become rich in a wrong way.

Harmony, peace, and tranquility is better than wealth

Better a small serving of vegetables with love, than a fattened calf with hatred. (Proverbs 15:17)

---

[265] McKane, quoted in Allan P. Ross "Proverbs" in *The Expositor's Bible Commentary, Proverbs-Isaiah, Vol. 6* Tremper Longman III and David E. Garland (eds.) (Grand Rapids, Michigan: Zondervan, 2008), 150.

[266] Hubbard, David A. *Proverbs* The Preacher's Commentary Series, Volume 15. (Nashville: Nelson, 1989), 348.

Better a dry crust with peace than a house full of feasting, with strife (Proverbs 17:1)

Besides wisdom and a good name, the book of Proverbs mentions a third value that is better than wealth, namely harmony, peace, and tranquility. Sometimes money can destroy relationships. We may dine in the most luxurious restaurants or have the best food on our tables at home, but at the same time our relationships are full of tension. How silly it is to spend more time and money on *what is on the table*, than on *who is around the table*. Money can put food on the table, but not fellowship around it, a house but not a home.[267]

If we eat our beef with strife, we have lost our perspective of what really counts in live. A wise person prefers eating bare beans with bonding, then baked beef with bitterness.

Good relationships are better than healthy food. Relationships are more important that material goods.

Having an intimate relationship with God is better than wealth

Better a little with the fear of the Lord, than great wealth with turmoil. (Proverbs 15:16)

A fourth thing that a wise person values more than wealth is having an intimate relationship with God. Not money, but our love for money, can easily damage our relationship with God. Fearing God, trusting Him to take care of us, submitting our being and having to His sovereign and loving authority will provide us with inner peace. On the other hand, however, great wealth, particularly our desire to have it or keep it, may result in turmoil, both within ourselves as well as in our families or communities. The turmoil caused by mammon manifests itself in 'the noisy, wild, stormy running and hunting about of the slave of mammon.'[268] A wise person values poverty and peace over wealth with worry. He values that what is more peaceful and fruitful eventually, namely an intimate relationship with the Lord, even if this means having less money on the bank.

Righteousness, honesty, integrity, justice is better than wealth

Wealth is worthless in the day of wrath, but righteousness delivers from death. (Proverbs 11:4)

---

[267] Waltke, I, 257.
[268] Delitzsch, quoted in Waltke, I, 627.

Better a little with righteousness than much gain with injustice. (Proverbs 16:8)

Better a poor whose walk is blameless than a fool whose lips are perverse. (Proverbs 19:1)

What a person desires is unfailing love, better to be poor than a liar. (Proverbs 19:22)

Better the poor person whose walk is blameless than the rich whose ways are perverse. (Proverbs 28:6)

Although money is not perverse, it not seldom leads its possessors into perverse ways or perverse lips, whether in their desire to obtain more or whether to avoid losing whatever wealth they have. Loyal love is better than wealth. A wise person is committed to honesty at all costs and to integrity whatever the result of it for their wealth. Someone's worth should not be measured by his bank account, but by his character expressed in justice, honesty, integrity, and righteousness. These characteristics are better than perversity, lying, injustice or oppression because they are blessed and protected by God.[269]

Humility is better than wealth

Better to be lowly in spirit along with the oppressed than to share plunder with the proud. (Proverbs 16:19)

Having wealth can give us an inflated sense of self-worth. It makes us less dependent on others, give us more power over our own life, to make our own decisions, to not be accountable to others. It might lead to seeing ourselves as being better and more valuable than those with less money. This can lead using our wealth to abuse people and oppress them. And before we know it, pride gets a prominent place in our life. Wealth can drive out meekness and humility from our hearts. When these characteristics are gone, we move towards the land of the fools. Wisdom is associated with meekness and humility, while God strongly condemns pride. Pride is a tendency to elevate us to a divine status. It goes against the mindset of fearing God, which as we have seen is the foundation of wisdom. Cultivating a humble spirit may not make us wealthy, but it will keep us in a right relationship with God.

---

[269] Proverbs 20:7; 2:7.

A wise person honors God with his wealth

Honor the Lord with your wealth, with the firstfruits of all your crops; then your barns will be filled to overflowing and your vats will brim over with new wine. (Proverbs 3:9,10)

Although a wise person knows that wealth is a relative value, that needs to be given its proper place considering other values, chances are that wise people have wealth. A wise person basic' characteristic is fear of God; therefore, it is inevitable that this expresses itself in his relationship to his wealth. The book of Proverbs gives us some guidelines as a how a wise person should use their wealth. The foundational thought is that a wise person honors the Lord with his wealth.

Honoring God means that we give Him the best of what we have. Giving to God means giving to causes that glorify Him, that extend His Name and rule on earth; giving to those, whether people or institutions, organizations, who serve Him.

Another aspect of honoring God with our wealth is to be grateful to Him for what we have received. He owns everything that is on, above, and in the earth. We are stewards of His wealth.

The book of Proverbs gives several other wise ways in which we can honor God with our wealth.

A wise person trusts in God and not in wealth for wisdom and security.

Those who trust in their riches will fall, but the righteous will thrive like a green leaf. (Proverbs 11:28)

The wealth of the rich is their fortified city, but poverty is the ruin of the poor. (Proverbs 10:15)

The name of the Lord is a strong tower, the righteous run to it and are safe. The wealth of the rich is their fortified city; they imagine it a wall too high to scale. (Proverbs 18:10,11)

The greedy stir up conflict, but those who trust in the Lord will prosper. (Proverbs 28:25)

A wise person honors God with his wealth because His trust remains in God and not in his wealth. We honor God by trusting Him.

A wise person is someone who understands that righteousness, one of the consequences of wisdom, and not wealth, provides a security that lasts beyond the grave. In the book of Proverbs we learn that wealth cannot buy innocence or acquittal before God, or buy off divine judgment.[270] The danger of wealth is that it provides a false sense of wisdom and security and might give its possessor an inflated sense of ability, power and confidence.[271] A wise person knows that it is the name of the Lord, signifying the attributes of God, that is a strong tower, or a fortified city, not one's wealth. One of the consequences for his daily life is that he does not need to be greedy for more wealth, nor cling to his possessions for security and significance, but can trust in the Lord. A wise person understands that riches are fleeting and temporary,[272] and therefore not suitable to build one's life upon.

Riches are not part of our identity and are external to a person. Wealth is subject to the winds of fortune and changes in circumstances. A wise person knows that if one trusts in wealth, he will fall, while trusting God will provides safety and security, which are not subject to changes in circumstances.

A wise person gives generously

All the day he (the sluggard) craves for more, but the righteous give without sparing. (Proverbs 21:26)

The generous will themselves be blessed, for they share their food with the poor. (Proverbs 22:9)

She opens her arms to the poor and extends her hands to the needy. (Proverbs 31:20)

The book of Proverbs finishes with a beautiful poem about a woman of noble character. She is a wise woman, who fears the Lord. She runs her household and her business in a way that honors the Lord. One of the things that is said about her is her generosity.[273] Generosity is a characteristic of God and therefore something that grows into people who fear Him. Of course, generosity is not limited to our material resources, but can also be applied to time, love, and service. A wise person does not give in to the temptation of cravings for

---

[270] "Wealth is worthless in the day of wrath, but righteousness delivers from death." (Proverbs 11:4)

[271] Proverbs 28:11.

[272] Proverbs 23:5; 27:24.

[273] Proverbs 31:20.

more for himself.[274] Generosity is an outflow of one's contentment with God and whatever He provides. It is walking by faith and not by sight. Throughout the book of Proverbs, one finds many examples of how generosity is part of the lives of those who are wise. We also find encouragements for the wise to maintain their generous lifestyle, as well as warnings against lack of generosity.[275] The wise who give generously often discover that they become richer, not poorer, both materialistically as well as spiritually.[276] On the other hand, those that serve Mammon instead of God become greedy and stingy, which makes them poorer in heart and relationally.[277]

A wise person uses his wealth to express kindness to the needy

The righteous care about justice for the poor, but the wicked have no such concern. (Proverbs 29:7)

It is a sin to despise one's neighbor but blessed is the one who is kind to the needy. (Proverbs 14:21)[278]

The generosity of the wise, particularly, but not only, extends to those in need. The Hebrew word used for 'generous' refers to 'a good eye.' A wise person has an eye for those in need. Their motive to use their wealth to bless those in need and improve their well-being, is to honor God and is an expression not only of their love for God, but also of the love of God that has become part of their lives because of their fear of God. They are kind, not only to people, but even to animals.[279] They treat what is weak and needy in an honorable way because God created them. They realize that the poor and those in need as equally made by God and should be treated with dignity, because God values them.[280] Despising them, by ignoring their needs or by withholding them kindness is to sin against God.[281] The wise extends their kindness also to enemies, going the extra mile to provide what they need.[282]

---

274 Proverbs 11:24–26.

275 Proverbs 3:27,28; 14:21; 19:17; 21:13; 22:9,22; 28:27.

276 Proverbs 11:24–26.

277 Proverbs 15:27; 28:22.

278 Others verses that express similar truths are Proverbs 19:17; 22:22,23; 21:13; 28:27.

279 Proverbs 12:10.

280 Proverbs 22:2.

281 Proverbs 14:31; 17:5.

282 Proverbs 25:21–22.

A wise person does not acquire wealth by unjust means nor uses wealth unjustly

Ill-gotten treasures have no lasting value, but righteousness delivers from death. (Proverbs 10:2)

The greedy bring ruin to their households, but the one who hates bribes will live. (Proverbs 15:27)

A fortune made by a lying tongue is a fleeting vapor and a deadly snare. (Proverbs 21:6)

Wealth in and of itself is not condemned by God, but He is extremely interested in how one acquires this wealth. He strongly disapproves of acquiring wealth by unjust or wicked means, such as violence,[283] oppression,[284] bribery,[285] dishonesty[286] or exorbitant interest.[287] A wise person, is someone who fears the Lord also in pursuing material wealth, and this means he will not give in to the temptation of becoming rich by means that are not approved by the living God.

Also, the wise person uses his wealth justly, which means he will act rightly and fairly in the economic sphere by using accurate weights and measures[288] and in dealings with inheritance.[289] A wise person does not use his wealth for involvement in risky financial enterprises.

> Proverbs devotes a considerable amount of teaching to warn the wise against securing loans for other people (6:1–5; 11:15; 17:18; 20:16; 22:26,27; 27:13; 28:8). … Charging interest was forbidden except to non-Israelites, but securing loans was thought to be a bad risk even in the case of the latter.[290]

---

283 Proverbs 1:10–19.

284 Proverbs 22:16.

285 Proverbs 15:27. A bribe is an illegitimate gift to encourage someone to act in a way that is wrong.

286 Proverbs 13:11; 21:6.

287 Proverbs 28:8.

288 Proverbs 11:1; 16:11; 20:10; 20:23.

289 Proverbs 22:28.

290 Sandoval, 111.

Will the wise become rich?

The wealth of the wise is their crown, but the folly of the fools yields folly. (Proverbs 14:24)

Humility is the fear of the Lord, its wages are riches and honor and life. (Proverbs 22:4)

The house of the righteous contains great treasure, but the income of the wicked brings ruin. (Proverbs 15:6)

Trouble pursues the sinner, but the righteous are rewarded with good things. (Proverbs 13:21)

When we pursue wisdom as our highest value, we might also become materially wealthy. When God asked Solomon what he wanted to receive, Solomon asked for wisdom. This was his first pursuit. But God was so pleased with this request that He also give him power and wealth (1 Kings 3:1–15). It is a matter of prioritizing. Jesus expressed something similar when He said: *"But seek first His Kingdom and his righteousness and all these things (referring to food, drink, clothing) will be given to you as well."* (Matthew 6:33)

Despite all that we have learned in this chapter about the relative value of wealth and the importance to honor God with our wealth, it is important to underline that the book of Proverbs has nothing against wealth. On the contrary, several verses suggest that wealth can be blessing from God for wise behavior.[291]

We have seen that wisdom is better than wealth, but immediately after Wisdom, personified as a woman, said that wisdom is more profitable than silver or gold[292] she suggests that wisdom brings material wealth.[293]

> It would not be unreasonable to assume ... that the one who finds wisdom would subsequently find these other things as well ... The not unreasonable assumption is that if Wisdom possesses wealth, then the one who finds wisdom will naturally attain wealth too.[294]

---

[291] Proverbs 3:9,10; 3:15,16; 10;22; 15:6.

[292] Proverbs 3:14,15; 8:18,19.

[293] Proverbs 3:16; 8:21.

[294] Sandoval, 81, 93.

The book of Proverbs does not condemn wealth. It does show that a wise person can also be wealthy. This can be the result of his wisdom, for example because he is diligent,[295] or because he restrains himself in using his money on trivialities;[296] or because he has inherited wealth[297] and, as we have already seen, because God blesses him.[298]

Nevertheless, the book of Proverbs also warns against the dangers of wealth, because it often breeds greed, pride, insensitivity, and inner turmoil. We need wisdom to handle wealth.

> Wisdom provides the recipient of increased finances with the restraints that are needed. Furthermore, it helps one maintain that essential equilibrium, for much wealth can be a heady trip. Since riches never make one honest, or generous or discerning, wisdom must come aboard to steer our vessel around those disastrous shallow reefs.[299]

The only prayer in the book of Proverbs that is a model prayer that can help us to navigate between the 'shallow reefs' of wealth:

> *Two things I ask of you, Lord, do not refuse me before I die:*
> *Keep falsehood and lies far from me; give me neither poverty nor riches but*
> *give me only my daily bread.*
> *Otherwise, I may have too much and disown you and say: 'Who is the Lord?'*
> *Or I may become poor and steal, and so dishonor the name of my God."*
> Proverbs 30:7–9

In this prayer, Agur prays that throughout his life God will prevent him from being deceitful, or self-sufficient. It is a prayer that God will not lead him into temptation, both of wealth and of poverty. He wants to honor God's name in all circumstances in his life. He wants to maintain integrity no matter what circumstances he is in. The prayer expresses his humility, his dependence upon God to maintain a wise and godly character, whether he has much or little. He also expresses self-knowledge, another characteristic of a wise person, and his own weakness to give in to the temptations associated with wealth, such as pride, arrogance and independence and the temptations associated with pov-

---

[295] Proverbs 10:4.

[296] Proverbs 21:17, 20.

[297] Proverbs 19:14.

[298] Proverbs 22:4.

[299] Swindoll, Charles. R. *Active Spirituality*. (Milton Keynes, Nelson Word Ltd., 1994), 193.

erty, such as stealing. Like Agur, it should be the desire of every wise person to live in contentment and trust between the extremes of poverty and wealth as a way of sanctifying the name or character of God.

We find echoes of this prayer of Agur in the prayer that Jesus taught His disciples and which has become known as the Lord's prayer.[300] In the context of teaching this prayer, Jesus speaks about giving to the needy,[301] how to deal with the temptations of riches[302] and poverty.[303] In this context Jesus taught us to pray that God will not lead us into temptation, that God will provide us with our daily bread and that God's Name will be glorified through our lives. These prayers of Agur and Jesus are timeless and the wise do well to make them part of their lives.

Questions for further reflection

1. In what way have you experienced that wealth can destroy relationships, both with God and with fellow human beings?

2. How do you honor God with your wealth?

3. In the book of Proverbs there are six values more important than wealth. What do you consider more valuable than wealth?

---

[300] Found in Matthew 6:9–13.

[301] Matthew 6:1–4.

[302] Matthew 6:19–24.

[303] Matthew 6:25–34.

CHAPTER 8
THE WISE MAN AND HIS MOUTH

Wise speech is rarer and more valuable than gold and rubies

(Proverbs 20:15 New Living Translation)

One of the ways we express our wisdom or folly is through our communication. If we keep silent all the time, we might be considered wise, while we really are a fool.

> *Even fools are thought wise if they keep silent, and discerning if they hold their tongues.* (Proverbs 17:28)

Unfortunately, we cannot hold our tongue forever, and once we start using it our wisdom or folly will show itself very soon. People that are considered wise are likely to be sought out for advice about life. Giving advice is often mentioned as one of the characteristics of a wise person.

It should not come as a surprise that a book that puts so much emphasis on wisdom, has a lot to say about the use of words. The book of Proverbs contains more than sixty one-liners about the use of the tongue. This underlines the importance of this topic when one thinks of wisdom. Being wise at heart will inevitably show in our speech.

> Skladny in a statistical analysis of themes in chapters 10:1–22:16 and 25–29 calculated that more than 20% of all proverbs in those chapters are concerned in one way or another with the spoken word and its power.[304]

High value placed on wisdom in communication

… for wisdom is more precious than rubies and nothing you desire can compare with it … (Proverbs 8:11)

The things we desire show what we value the most. God wants us to value wisdom more than anything else, because there is nothing else that will honor Him more than that we live our lives in the fear of the LORD, which is the foundation of wisdom.

---

[304] Whybray, 140.

Placing such a high value of wisdom in general is followed by placing a high value of wise communication.

> *Gold there is, and rubies in abundance but lips that speak knowledge are a rare jewel.* (Proverbs 20:15)

> *The tongue of the righteous is choice silver ...* (Proverbs 10:20)

Wise communication is like a precious jewel

A word aptly spoken is like apples of gold in settings of silver. Like an earring of gold or an ornament of fine gold is a wise man's rebuke to a listening ear. (Proverbs 25:11,12)

Wise communication is compared to a rare jewel, more precious than gold and rubies, choice silver and an elegant and custom-made piece of jewelry. It is a rare and precious ornament and therefore extremely valuable and should be treasured and desired above anything else.

> The phrase, to judge from the parallel, here refers to a beautifully finished piece of jewelry perhaps made of gold and coral for the face ... The metaphor expresses the unstated thought that lips ... that speak knowledge are extremely valuable and aesthetically pleasing and the unstated feeling that they are earnestly desired. Although comparative particles are missing, the precious vessel is implicitly better than gold and corals because, beyond consisting of these most precious materials, it is finely wrought and exquisitely manufactured. Thought-through speech that conforms to God-established morality presupposes the long hard work of education that is finally more precious than all possible materials. It is incomparably superior to any treasure ...[305]

Wise lips are a piece of art wrought by the Almighty God in the lives of those who are committed to fearing Him. Knowing that having a wise tongue is a priceless, might stir up our desire to make this part of our lives. Having a wise tongue expresses itself in several key aspects.

A wise person speaks gently

Wisdom in our communicating is not only noticed in the kind of words we use, but particularly in the *tone* with which we use our words. A wise person speaks with patience and gentleness. A wise person uses a gentle tone.

---

[305] Waltke, II, 144.

A gentle answer turns away wrath, but a harsh word stirs up anger. (Proverbs 15:1)

The wise in heart are called discerning, and gracious words make a person persuasive. (Proverbs 16:21)

Through patience a ruler can be persuaded, and a gentle tongue can break a bone. (Proverbs 25:15)[306]

Our patient, gentle and calm tone has enormous influence. It can break down strong opposition and it can turn away wrath and bring about reconciliation. A soft or tender response helps social cohesion in a community and is one that maintains and promotes relationships. It is important to know how to interact wisely during a disagreement or argument. A friendly, mild answer allow tempers to cool. A wise person can defuse a tense situation with gentle, patient words. Gracious words can break down the deepest, most hardened resistance to an idea.

A wise person uses his words with restraint

The one who has knowledge uses words with restraint and whoever has understanding is even-tempered. (Proverbs 17:27)

Knowing that words can hurt and that a word once spoken cannot be recalled, a wise person restrains his or her speech when imparting knowledge[307] or when wronged.[308]

A wise person is *discrete* in his communication. He does not betray a secret.[309] He or she knows it is not wise to be gossiping, because this can destroy relationships and communities. Gossiping is unloving and violates God's command to love one's neighbor. It is a form of despising, belittling the other person because of real or imagined flaws or mistakes. A wise person therefore keeps silent.

---

[306] Other verses that express a similar thought: Proverbs 12:16; 14:29; 15:18.

[307] "The prudent keep their knowledge to themselves, but a fool's heart blurts out folly." (12:23) see also 10:14.

[308] "Sin is not ended by multiplying words, but the prudent hold their tongues." (10:19).

[309] "Whoever derides their neighbor has no sense, but the one who has understanding holds their tongue. A gossip betrays a confidence, but a trustworthy person keeps a secret." (11:12,13)

"Whoever would foster love coves over an offense, but whoever repeats the matter, separates close friends." (17:9)

A wise person speaks *thoughtfully.* A wise person is a careful listener, who reflects, thinks, and listens before he speaks. A wise person does not make promises under the inspiration of the hour. A wise person weights and measures his words. He avoids blurring out without regard for accuracy, circumstance, audience, or emotions. A wise person has the inner capacity to reflect, rather than react emotionally. Someone who is wise is considerate and has the self-control to reflect and not to act emotionally.[310]

A wise person knows when and how to *control* their tongue.[311] Their aim is to promote harmony and love, and this means they know the importance of overlooking an insult.

A wise person speaks in a timely manner

A person finds joy in giving an apt reply – and how good is a timely word. (Proverbs 15:23)

Wise communication is not only to use our words with restraint and in a gentle tone, but an important aspect of wise communication is also to say the right word at the right time.

To speak at the right time in the right way to the right person is a priceless virtue. Sometimes, we say what is right, but it might not be an appropriate moment to say it. How precious when a comment or a response is spoken in a timely manner. As we have seen a worthwhile and valuable word can be like 'an apple of gold' but when spoken at the right time it is as if this golden apple is placed in a setting of silver, which enhances its value.[312] A wise person reads the circumstances and the people he or she is dealing with and chooses his words accordingly. Seizing the moment is a hallmark of wisdom. We read of Daniel, who spoke "with wisdom and tact" (Daniel 2:13) in a delicate situation that might have cost his life. But his wise words saved not only his own life, but that of many others.

---

[310] To answer before listening, that is folly and shame (18:13) It is a trap to dedicate something rashly, and only later to consider one's vows. (20:25) A false witness will perish, but a careful listener will testify successfully. (21:28) The heart of the righteous weighs its answers, but the mouth of the wicked gushes evil. (15:28)

[311] "Those who guard their mouths and their tongues, keep themselves from calamity." (21:23) "Those who guard their lips, preserve their lives, but those who speak rashly will come to ruin." (13:3) Other verses that express a similar thought: Proverbs 12:16; 29:20.

[312] Proverbs 25:11.

A wise person speaks beneficially

Through the blessing of the upright a city is exalted, but by the mouth of the wicked it is destroyed. (Proverbs 11:11).

We all know, mostly from experience, that words can pierce like swords. Words can damage and destroy relationships, communities, even whole cities. The book of Proverbs recognizes this. Our words have enormous power. They can provide life, vitalization, encouragement, lifting our spirits, but unfortunately, our words can also kill relationships, confidence, trust, bonds.[313]

Most of us have experienced some of this power. We can lift people up with encouraging words, but hurtful words stay with us for many years. A well-known and popular expression states: "Sticks and stones can break my bones, but words will never hurt me." Nevertheless, many of us have experienced the harm caused by words. Just think back on some of hurtful things that have been said to you over the years, whether by teachers, parents, a brother or a sister, friends, school mates, spouse, colleagues, etc. It might have impacted your feelings, hopes and ambitions, and sense of self-worth. These comments may still linger in your mind.

> A slip of the foot you may soon recover, but a slip of the tongue you may never get over.[314]

But words cannot only hurt, they can also edify, enlighten, educate, nourish, unite, invigorate, soothe, bring peace and hope. Good community depends on wise communication.

The book of Proverbs considers the tongue of the wise as an organ for providing healing, bringing peace and harmony, and spreading knowledge.[315]

---

[313] "The tongue has the power of life and death, and those who love it will eat its fruit." (Proverbs 18:21) "With their mouths the godless destroy their neighbors ..." (Proverbs 11:9)

[314] Benjamin Franklin, quoted in Anders, Proverbs, 218.

[315] "The mouth of the righteous is a fountain of life ..." (10:11); "The lips of the righteous nourish many ..." (10:21); "... the tongue of the wise brings healing." (12:18); "A king's wrath is messenger of death, but the wise will appease it." (16:14); "Gracious words are a honeycomb, sweet to the soul and healing to the bones." (16:24); "Mockers stir up a city, but the wise turn away anger." (29:8)

The words of the wise come from his heart

The tongue of the righteous is choice silver, but the heart of the wicked is of little value. (Proverbs 10:20)

We have seen the value, importance, and main characteristic of wise communication and this might have stirred up our desire to speak wisely always and everywhere and always avoid foolish communication. But how can this be? The answer to this question seems strange. The best way to grow in wise communication is to take care of our heart.

In the book of Proverbs there is a clear connection between one's mouth, one's tongue, and one's heart.[316] In the book of Proverbs, the word 'heart' stands for one's core personality, one's character. The heart produces the words, and the words reveal the heart. The inward 'heart' and the outward 'mouth' complement each other.

> The mouth is ... the direct conduit to and from the heart. On the one hand, it allows one to test firsthand what is going on in the heart.[317]

Our words reveal our character. Our words reflect what is going on inside. Our inward heart expresses itself in our lips that speak.

> Speech is the index of the mind.[318]

> The heart of fools is in their mouths; but the mouth of the wise is in their heart.[319]

The source of wise communication is the character of a person, who is committed to fearing God and seeks to know Him in all his ways and all her decisions. Such a person is considered 'righteous' in the words of the book of Proverbs and wisdom is a fruit that grows out of this.[320]

---

[316] One of the characteristics of Hebrew poetry is parallelism, which refers to the correspondence of the first half of the line, or verse with the second half. For example: *"The lips* of the wise spread knowledge, but *the hearts* of fools are not upright." (15:7); *"The discerning heart* seeks knowledge, but *the mouth* of a fool feeds on folly." (15:14) Other examples of this connection between heart and tongue, lips are found in Proverbs 15:28, 16:21; 16:23; 17:20; 23:15,16; 24:1,2.

[317] Waltke 299, 300.

[318] Seneca, the Roman philosopher of the first century AD quoted in Waltke, I 480.

[319] Sirach 21:26 quoted in Waltke, I, 471.

[320] From the mouth of the righteous comes the fruit of wisdom ... (Proverbs 10:31a).

The mouth of the righteous produces wisdom. Of the woman who fears God it is said: "She speaks with wisdom and faithful instruction is on her tongue." (Proverbs 31:26)

What a man says wells up from what he is. Therefore, we are encouraged to keep our heart with all vigilance.

> Above all else, guard your heart, for everything you do flows from it. Keep your mouth free from perversity; keep corrupt talk far from your lips. (Proverbs 4:23,24)

If you guard your heart, it will be a lot easier to guard your tongue. Wise speech comes from a wise heart.

> If the seat of spiritual capacities (heart) is not in order, then no knowledge can be expected from the lips.[321]

Conclusion

A fool's mouth lashes out with pride, but the lips of the wise protect them. (Proverbs 14:3)

Wise communication is not only pleasing to God and beneficial to others, but also valuable for yourself,[322] because "A fool's tongue is long enough to cut his own throat."[323]

Questions for further reflection

1. We read in the Bible that "if anyone is never at fault with what he says, he is a perfect man ..." (James 3:2). How do you try to keep your tongue, to say the right thing at the right time, always?

2. What is the most beautiful compliment you have ever received? What is the most hurtful thing someone has ever said to you?

3. How many compliments do you give each day? How can you increase this number?

---

[321] Waltke, 620.

[322] "With their mouths the godless destroy their neighbors, but through knowledge the righteous escape." (11:9); "The words of the wicked lie in wait for blood, but the speech of the upright rescues them." (12:6).

[323] Waltke, 102.

CHAPTER 9
THE WISE MAN AND HIS FRIENDS

A genuine friend is a gift of God's mercy to you[324]

A wise person knows the value of friendship.

The book of Proverbs underlines that wisdom is relational. Wisdom not only develops when our relationship with God deepens, but also grows in interaction with others, like parents, one's spouse, friends, and with the wise.[325]

The book of Proverbs has several proverbs where the word 'friend', 'friendship', 'neighbor' is used.[326] It is not always obvious, whether $r\bar{e}^a$', the term that is used, refers to a neighbor or to a friend.

> The most commonly used word for 'friend' and 'neighbor' is the noun $r\bar{e}^a$' which is formed from the verb r'h (to associate with). The noun thus refers to another person with whom one is close. The translation 'friend' indicates emotional attachment, while 'neighbor' fits those contexts where spatial intimacy is meant. Surely the two sometimes overlap and in some contexts it proves difficult to decide between 'neighbor' and 'friend' as the best English translation ... at times our translation 'friend' might be bettered rendered 'neighbor' and vice versa.[327]

Many years ago, I met with a Christian leader who was about to retire. He was a spiritual man, who had a close relationship with God. One comment he made, stuck with me. He said: *"I'm about to retire and will have time to spend with friends, but I hardly have any friends!"* Here was a man, who was used by God, who loved God with all his heart, who had given his life to serving God, but too late he realized that he had neglected an important part of his life, namely developing meaningful friendships with other men.

---

[324] Stanley, Charles. *Walking Wisely*. (Nashville, Tennessee: Thomas Nelson, 2002), 139.

[325] "Walk with the wise and become wise ..." (13:20).

[326] 3:27–31; 6:1–5; 11:9,12; 14:20; 16:29; 17:9,17,18; 18:17,24; 19:4,6,7; 20:6; 21:10; 22:11; 23:10,11; 24:28,29; 25:8–10,17,18; 26:18,19; 27:9,10,14,17.

[327] Tremper Longman III. *Proverbs*. Baker Commentary on the Old Testament Wisdom and Psalms. (Grand Rapids MI: Baker Academic, 2006), 555.

Unfortunately, he is not alone. In the book *Friendship Factor,* the author points out that only about ten percent of men have real friends. In answer to the question why this is so, he writes

> One simple reason: We do not devote ourselves sufficiently to it. If our relationships are the most valuable commodity we can own in this world, one would expect that everyone would assign friendship highest priority. ... Significant relationships come to those who assign them enough importance to cultivate them.[328]

It is foolish to think that we can go through life without meaningful relationships with other human beings, even when we have a close relationship with God. Also, people who have a strong marriage relationship need other friends besides their spouse. Most women understand this, while men are struggling with this. For his well-being a man needs several good male friends and for her well-being a woman needs several good female friends. We might need various kinds of friends.

In his book *Vital Friends,* Tom Rath, identifies eight vital roles that friends bring to our lives: builder, champion, collaborator, companion, connector, energizer, mind opener, navigator.[329]

In his book *When Men Think Private Thoughts,* Gordon MacDonald gives a helpful description of four distinct kinds of friendships: 1) A friend, who wants to enjoy and explore life with you; 2) A friend who looks deep into your life and sees what he needs. 3) A mentor friend, who is not afraid to tell you where you need to improve, and who helps you to grow and learn; 4) A friend, who keeps you accountable, but also ready to help when you are helpless and broken.[330]

We are wise when we realize how valuable friends are.

> A friend loves you unconditionally, catches you when you fall, believes in the best for you and encourages the best in you, shares your deepest concerns applauds your successes and feels your pain, offers you con-

---

[328] McGinnis, Alan Loy. *The Friendship Factor: how to get closer to the people you care for.* (Minneapolis: Augsburg Publishing House, 1979), 25.

[329] For more information and elaboration of each of these roles see: Tom Rath *Vital Friends: The People You Can't Afford to Live Without.* (New York: Gallup Press, 2006).

[330] MacDonald, Gordon. *When Men Think Private Thoughts.* (Nashville, Tennessee: Thomas Nelson Inc., 1997), 166–179.

structive criticism in times of error and feels sorrow for you in times of pain or rejection.[331]

In the book of Proverbs, the value of friendship is underlined by its use of three metaphors.

A friend is like a delightful perfume

Perfume and incense bring joy to the heart, and the pleasantness of a friend springs from their heartfelt advice (Proverbs 27:9) Just as lotions and fragrance give sensual delight, a sweet friendship refreshes the soul. (27:9, The Message)

The council/advice that a faithful friend provides is like a delightful perfume. It sweetens our life and makes us pleasant to be around. Like perfume, a good friend brings joy, pleasure, and delight. A good friendship refreshes the soul as perfume refreshes the body.

As we put on perfume to feel good and to make us pleasant to be around, so the council and company of a good friend provides us with joy and pleasure and makes us a better person socially.

The council of a friend is pleasant as perfume because it comes from someone who knows us, loves us, and has our best interests in mind. "Loving, solicitous council on the part of a faithful friend is as refreshing and stimulating to the soul as oil and perfume are to the body."[332]

Although a friend him or herself can already be a delightful perfume, a refreshing oil, what makes this friendship particularly sweet is the advice, support, and encouragement that such a friend provides. A good friend makes us a better person.

As perfume can be costly, so a good friendship is valuable and needs to be treated with care.

Oil, perfume, and incense are often associated with pleasure, joy, and feasting. This is also what true friendship provides. The good counsels of a friend sweeten our soul.

---

[331] Stanley, *Walking Wisely*, 19.

[332] Ironside, H.A. *Proverbs*. (Neptune, New Jersey: Loizeaux Brothers, 1996) 223.

A friend is like iron sharpening iron

As iron sharpens iron so one person sharpens another. (Proverbs 27:17)

A loyal friend not only provides a refreshing advice and support, but also a sharp rebuke. The second metaphor that is used in the book of Proverbs to underline the value of friendship is that of 'sharpening iron'. To sharpen an iron instrument, another iron instrument is used. Rubbed with each other by friction, they become sharper and polished.

As people in sports or education sharpen their physical or mental abilities through interacting with fellow athletes or fellow students/teachers, likewise good friends can refine us and make us grow in character. When we rub shoulders with good friends, we are also rubbing hearts. The rabbis applied it to students: 'Just as iron sharpens iron so does the intellect become keener by contact with other intellects.'[333]

Our friends function as 'sharpening iron' when they challenge our weaknesses. They might say or do things that hurt us, but these are wounds of a friends, administered out of love.

> Better is open rebuke than hidden love. Faithful are the wounds of a friend, profuse are the kisses of an enemy." (Proverbs 27:5,6)

Devoted friends do not shy away from constructive criticism. The result of having a friend 'hard as iron' is that we grow in character and in our obedience to God. Sometimes a good friend must speak plainly and plain words to correct a mistake, protect us from faults or restore a broken relationship. His or her disapproval seeks to help us avoid deviating from the right path. We need such tough love to navigate through live successfully.

We need such friends.

> A loving friend is intended to help us, to improve us in our walk with God. He may help us by giving us heartening encouragement and demonstrating genuine affection. Equally, as we see here, he may help us by taking up and applying the scalpel, as needed. His cuts, however, are intended to bring long-term healing, even though they may bring short-term pain.[334]

---

[333] Quoted by Waltke, footnote 67, Waltke II, 384.

[334] Phillips, 182.

Henry Alford, NT scholar from the 19th century called the giving of Christian rebuke "the best and most difficult office of Christian friendship."[335]

> The influence of a wise friend can sharpen one's discernment, perspective, and insight in ways that one could not achieve by individual efforts.[336]

A friend is like reflecting water

As water reflects the face, so others reflect your heart back to you. (Proverbs 27:19)

Besides the delightful perfume of his sweet council and the tough love of the sharp iron, the book of Proverbs uses a third metaphor to express the value of friendship, namely that of water reflecting our face.

The idea is that when we look in the water our face is reflected, we see ourselves in a different light. Unlike a mirror, which provides a predictable reflection, the surface of the water is ever changing, showing a variety of 'ourselves.' Also, unlike a mirror, the reflection in water implies depth. This seems to an be apt image of true friendship.

> When people engage in rigorous interaction with others who reflect them, offer counter ideas, express alternatives, or just listen, they discover new insights. Thoughts are clarified.[337]

I have often experienced that those friends help me crystallize my thinking. When I verbalize my thoughts with friends, my understanding of the idea often deepens. A friend reflects my mind. Not seldom a friend can plumb the depts of my thoughts.

> The purposes of a person's heart are deep waters, but one who has insight draws them out. (Proverbs 20:5)

Self-reflection in the presence of trusted friends can be enormously enriching. Sometimes we only have thoughts that we have not found words for to describe.

---

[335] Alford, Henry. *Alford's Greek Testament: An Exegetical and Critical Commentary.* (Bellingham, WA: Logos Research Systems Inc., 2010).

[336] Estes, Daniel J. *Handbook on the Wisdom books and Psalms.* (Grand Rapids, Michigan: Baker Academic, 2005), 239.

[337] Bland, 100.

> The thought process is not complete until the idea is verbalized, meaning that, until individuals can explain or express their thoughts to others, they do not understand them as well as they think.[338]

Interacting with a trusted friend can help us verbalize our deep and inner thoughts and clarify our motives.

> The image is of a deep well. It takes a person with a bucket and long rope to draw out the water. In the same way, it takes time, patience, and one who is indeed a friend to plumb the depths of another's thoughts.[339]

An old German maxim says, 'the best mirror is an old friend.'[340]

It is a sign of real friendship when a friend can discern our deepest intentions, even when these are not yet fully verbalized. It is an immense joy and encouragement when a friend can provide fresh insight into our thoughts and to bring to surface what is in our mind.

A wise person chooses her friends carefully

The righteous choose their friends carefully, but the way of the wicked leads them astray. (Proverbs 12:26)

A wise person not only values friendships, but he or she recognizes the enormous influence friends have and selects friends carefully.

> Because of the significant effects that friends produce in those who are close to them, to a large degree the friends we choose determine what kind of people we become. Consequently, we must choose our friends wisely, for in choosing them we are likely choosing our own future.[341]

Sometimes it is said that we become like those whom we like. This might mean that we take on some characteristics of those whom we trust and admire. Taking this into consideration makes us careful in choosing our friends.

An English proverb says: "Tell me who are your friends, and I will tell you who you are."[342] Our friends influence us, more than we sometimes realize.

---

338 Ibid.

339 Ibid.

340 Ibid.

341 Estes, 239.

342 Miguel de Cervantes included the saying in the second part of his celebrated Spanish opus "Don Quixote" in 1615. The character Sancho Panza delivered the line

Walk with the wise and become wise for a companion of fools suffers harm.
(Proverbs 13:20)

Knowing about the value of wisdom and the joy of having loyal friends, we
should not overlook the possibility that there are fair-weather, inauthentic
'friends' who are more interested in our money, our favors or influence, than
in us and who we are.[343]

The book of Proverbs is aware of such credulous friends and warns us against
others whose company we need to avoid when we want to grow in being a
wise person, who is: a person who navigates his/her life in accordance with
the will of the Sovereign and Loving Creator.

Fools should not be our friends

Walk with the wise and become wise, for a companion of fools suffers harm.
(13:20)

Stay away from a fool, for you will not find knowledge on their lips. (14:7)

People that are considered 'fools' in the eyes of God will not help us becoming
wise and should not become part of our circle of friends. Fools as Proverbs describes them are arrogant, not open to correction, and lack the fear of God,
which we want to grow in, when we want to be wise. Best not to have fools in
our circle of close friends.

We should avoid a close friendship with a hot-tempered person

> Do not make friends with a hot-tempered person, do not associate with
> one easily angered, or you may learn their ways and get yourself en-
> snared. (Proverbs 22:24,25)

A hot-tempered person who is not able to control his temper will not be a
good friend. He or she has not learned to trust God to settle scores for
him/her and acts as if he/she is God. If we spend too much time with them,
their anger might develop an angry spirit in us and the way she expresses her
anger, might become the way we express our anger.

---

while indicating that it was a pre-existing proverb. https://quoteinvestigator.com/
2020/04/04/company-keep.

[343] "The poor are shunned even by their neighbors, but the rich have many friends."
(14:20); "Wealth attracts many friends …" (19:4); "Many curry favor with a ruler,
and everyone is the friend of one who gives gifts." (19:6)

We should not make friends with people that have 'mouth-problems'

A gossip betrays a confidence, so avoid anyone who talks too much. (Proverbs 20:19)

Like a broken tooth or a lame foot is reliance on the unfaithful in a time of trouble. (Proverbs 25:19)

Do not envy the wicked, do not desire their company, for their hearts plot violence and their lips talk about making trouble. (Proverbs 24:1,2)

Also, if we want to be wise, we should not develop or maintain friendships with people that have 'mouth-problems'. This could be people that are gossiping, lying, or given to flattering. Remember: they that gossip about others in your presence, will highly likely gossip about you when they are with others.

We should not develop a friendship with people who lack self-control

Do not join those who drink too much wine, or gorge themselves on meat, for drunkards and gluttons become poor and drowsiness clothes them in rags. (Proverbs 23:20)

Lastly, we want to grow in wisdom, we should not be friends with people who structurally lack control over their desires, whether for lust, wealth, drink, or people that have a rebellious spirit.[344]

A wise person knows how to maintain a friendship

Knowing how valuable friendship is and what significant role friends play in our lives as God's gift to us to help us grow spiritually, mentally, and emotionally, and towards becoming a wiser man or woman, should encourage us to consider our friends as precious treasures with whom we need to maintain a healthy relationship. We must keep our friendship in constant repair. The book of Proverbs gives some clear guidelines on what this means.

---

[344] "The accomplices of thieves are their own enemies; they are put under oath and dare not testify." (29:24); "A discerning son heeds instruction, but a companion of gluttons disgraces his father." (28:7); "A man who loves wisdom brings joy to his father, but a companion of prostitutes squanders his wealth." (29:2); "Fear the Lord and the king, my son and do not join with rebellious officials." (24:21)

A wise person invests in friendships

> Do not forsake your friend, or a friend of your family, and do not go to
> your relative's house when disaster strikes you – better a neighbor
> nearby than a relative far away. (Proverbs 27:10)

No relationship thrives without investing time and energy into it, and our
friendship relation is no exception. We need to cultivate and cherish the
friendship relationship.

A wise person does not take advantage of friendships

*Seldom set foot in your neighbor's house – too much of you, and they will hate
you.* (Proverbs 25:17)

In maintaining our friendship, it is important to 'not overstay our welcome.'
We need to know when to go. It is better when our friend wants to see more
of us, rather than less of us.

> Solomon's point is not *never* to spend a lot of time with a friend. Ra-
> ther, he is counseling us to spend the time appropriate to the friend-
> ship, to nurture and cultivate it without saturating and drowning it. This
> calls for consideration and sensitivity.[345]

Wisdom is knowing when we are welcome and when we are not. This requires
sensitivity to the feelings of our friend. The leads to the next suggestion in
maintaining a healthy friendship, namely

A wise person relates to her friend with tact and sensitivity

*If anyone loudly blesses their neighbor early in the morning, it will be taken as
a curse.* (Proverbs 27:14)

Frequent conversation is an important part of maintaining our friendship.
Wise communication involves not only *what* we say, but *how* and *when* and
why we say it. There are morning and evening people. A morning person is
right awake the minute she gets out of bed, while the evening person is a slow
starter. In a healthy friendship relation with an evening person, we need to be
sensitive to his early morning mood. Such sensitivity can expand to all areas of
life. A blessing is normally received well, provided the timing is right. Saying
the right thing at the wrong time or in the wrong manner can be perceived as

---

[345] Phillips, 177.

a curse, not a blessing. The Italians say: "He who praises you more than he is wont to do, either has deceived you, or is about to do it."[346]

> Job's "friends" illustrate with their unhelpful reactions to his troubles, the damage that can be done when limited human wisdom is combined with a lack of insight and sensitivity to another's need. With the best of intentions, but with incomplete wisdom, they diagnose his problem to the best of their ability and are terribly wrong in their conclusions.[347]

Chuck Swindoll gave the following description of a best friend: "A best friend is someone who knows enough to ruin you – and doesn't."[348]

A wise person knows when to let go of offenses

Whoever would foster love covers over an offense, but whoever repeats a matter separates close friends. (17:9) Hatred stirs up conflict, but love covers over all wrongs. (Proverbs 10:12)

A good friendship creates vulnerability, and this allows the other to hurt us. In any friendship there will be tense situations or times that our friend unintentionally offends us. It is important that we learn to deal with this in a loving and forgiving way. If we do not manage the offenses wisely, we could cause serious harm in the friendship relationship.

A wise person is a faithful friend

A friend loves at all times, and a brother is born for a time of adversity. (Proverbs 17:17)

Many claim to have unfailing love, but a faithful person who can find? (Proverbs 20:6)

It is great *to have* a faithful, loyal friend, and equally important it is for us *to be* a faithful, loyal friend. Faithfulness is a characteristic of God and should therefore also be part of the character of someone who fears Him.

In this time of social media, we might have hundreds or even thousands of friends. But most of these are superficial relationships and would not qualify

---

[346] Quoted by Ironside, 224.

[347] Curtis and Brugaletta, 117.

[348] Chuck Swindoll from a broadcast sermon, quoted in Dan Phillips "God's Wisdom in Proverbs", 174.

for the kind of friend that 'sticks closer than a brother.'[349] We might suffer from 'friendship inflation', having many casual acquaintances that cannot be counted on and who would not always loving. Better to have a few faithful friends, who stand by us through thick and thin.

A friend is one who walks in, when others walk out.[350]

Conclusion

A fitting conclusion to this chapter about the wise and his friends is this beautiful description of a friend

A friend should be radical.
He should love you when you're unlovable,
hug you when you're unhuggable,
and bear with you when you're unbearable.
A friend should be fanatical.
He should cheer you when the whole world boos,
dance when you get good news,
and cry when you cry, too.

But most of all a friend should be mathematical.
He should multiply the joy, divide the sorrow,
subtract the past, and add to tomorrow,
calculate the need deep in your heart,
and always be bigger than the sum of all their parts.[351]

Questions for further reflection

1. How many good friends do you have? How would you describe this friendship?

2. Are you involved in friendship relations that do you more harm than good? If so, what steps will you take to change this?

3. For whom are you a best friend and how can you strengthen this relationship?

---

[349] "One who has unreliable friends soon comes to ruin, but there is a friend who sticks closer than a brother." (Proverbs 18:24)

[350] Walter Winchell, (1897–1972). Winchell was an American newspaper columnist and radio news commentator. https://www.goodreads.com/quotes/179221-a-friend-is-one-who-walks-in-when-others-walk.

[351] Stanley, 156.

CHAPTER 10
THE WISE MAN AND HIS SPOUSE

Houses and wealth are inherited from parents,
but a prudent wife is from the Lord.
(Proverbs 19:14)

Solomon, who wrote and collected most of the proverbs in the Book of Proverbs, might be considered an expert on marriage because he had seven hundred wives and three hundred concubines! Nevertheless, in this part of his life he was not the wisest man on earth. The verdict of the Word of God about Solomon in this regard is truly clear:

> King Solomon … loved many foreign women beside Pharaoh's daughter – Moabites, Ammonites, Edomites, Sidonians and Hittites. They were from the nations about which the Lord had said the Israelites, "You must not intermarry with them, because they will surely turn your hearts after their gods." Nevertheless, Solomon held fast to them in love. He had seven hundred wives of royal birth and three hundred concubines, and his wives led him astray. As Solomon grew old his wives turned his heart after other gods and his heart was not fully devoted to the Lord his God … (1 Kings 11:1–6)

This testimony about Solomon is a good illustration that one cannot disobey a clear command from God without severe consequences. God wants to be honored and obeyed, especially in our marriage. A wise man and a wise woman listens to God's advice about their marriage.

Although, Solomon, who penned most of the proverbs we will look at below, did not obey his own principles to the end of his life, nevertheless his words have, through providence of the Sovereign Lord, found their place in the Holy Scriptures because they are "God-breathed … and useful for teaching, rebuking, correcting and training in righteousness …" (2 Timotheus 3:16)

The book of Proverbs has some good things to say about entering and maintaining a marriage that reflects the wisdom of God. Proverbs is often considered a kind of catechism for young men, to prepare them for a God-honoring role in their family and in society. That is why it addresses men more specifically and has more references to wives than to husbands. But we can apply the same verses that are written to husbands and substitute the word 'wife' in the verses below with 'spouse', without violating the principles behind the statements.

What follows are five guiding principles for entering and maintaining a marriage as a wise man or a wise woman.

Choose our spouse wisely: it is our crown or your cancer

A wife of noble character is her husband's crown, but a disgraceful wife is like decay in his bones. (Proverbs 12:4)

Choosing a spouse is one of the most important decisions in our life. It will have lifelong consequences, be it good or bad.[352]

Our spouse is one of the most influential people in our life. She can be our crown that brings us honor, or he can put us to shame. He can bring the best out of us or can she eat our personality away. Our spouse can invigorate us with encouragements and support or can infect us with negativism. Our spouse can make or break us and make our life like heaven or like hell.

We have seen from Solomon's life that his wives had such an influence on him that they drove him away from following God with all his heart.

We see the influence of a spouse also in the life of another important believer: Job. When Job was struggling with difficulties in his life, he did not get much support from his wife, when she told him: "Are you still maintaining your integrity? Curse God and die." (Job 2:9). She was talking like a foolish woman, or to use the metaphor of Proverbs, as someone who was like decay in his bones.

Our spouse can strengthen our walk with God or hinder us from following Him with all our heart. This should make us ask for wisdom in choosing the right partner. A partner is one of the gifts that God might want to give us.

He who finds a wife finds what is good and receives favor from the Lord. (Proverbs 18:22)

Houses and wealth are inherited from parents, but a prudent wife is from the Lord. (Proverbs 19:14)

---

[352] "A wife of noble character who can find? She is worth far more than rubies. Her husband has full confidence in her and lacks nothing of value. She brings him good, not harm, all the days of her life." (Proverbs 31:10)

Part of being a wise man and a wise woman is to choose his or her spouse wisely, that is carefully and prayerfully. For some, it is part of God's wisdom for their lives that they do not get married. Fearing Him in this circumstance is to trust His wisdom and ask for His strength and companionship.

Cultivate a strong intimate relationship with our spouse and be intoxicated with his/her love

Drink water from your own cistern, running water from your own well. Should your springs overflow in the streets, your streams of water in the public squares? Let them be yours alone, never to be shared with strangers. May your fountain be blessed, and may you rejoice in the wife of your youth. A loving doe, a graceful deer – may her breasts satisfy you always, may you ever be intoxicated with her love. (Proverbs 5:15–19)

One of the joys of marriage is having an intimate and strong relationship with another human being, who is given to us by our Creator to collaborate with us to accomplish His purpose in this world and to serve Him joyfully and fruitfully.

The Bible tells us that God created woman as 'a helper suitable' for the man (Genesis 2:18). This term 'helper' is sometimes used for God and therefore should not be taken to mean 'slave' or 'subordinate'. It refers to someone who comes alongside.

> That word helper in the language of the Old Testament, carries with it the idea of doing something for someone that he lacks the skill to do.[353]

The word 'suitable' can be translated as 'corresponding to him' and as such includes the idea of being complementary. Our spouse complements us and collaborates with us to fulfill our life calling.

God created one man and one woman, and His ideal is that a marriage consists of one husband and one wife. The fact that many great Bible characters (including Abraham, David, and Solomon) had more than one wife deviates from God's original intention. He has tolerated this, although from their stories in the Bible we learn that such polygamous relationships resulted in more 'curses' than 'blessings.'

---

[353] Smally, Gary & John Trent, *The Language of Love: How to Quickly Communicate your Feelings and Needs.* (Wheaton, Illinois, Tyndale House Publishers, 1988), 37.

Given the fact that Solomon himself (at least later in life) could not be faithful to one wife, but had to have about a thousand, it is stunning that he has put together several proverbs that clearly warn against infidelity in marriage.[354] Perhaps in the early part of his life he abided by those principles, but he was not willing to pursue this till the end. If only, he had lived by his own principles, he would not only have lived as a wise man, but died as one, also.

Nevertheless, one of the lessons that God passed on to us through Solomon was that one of the best ways to protect ourselves and our spouse from infidelity is to cultivate a strong intimate relationship with each other.

Proverbs 5:15–19 speaks of 'being intoxicated with our spouse's love.' Among other things this refers to the exhilarating joy of sex within marriage. It is compared with drinking from our own cistern. We need to consider our spouse as our God-given well of joy, pleasure, intimacy and good-will. Our spouse is given to us to fulfill our sexual needs.

One way to cultivate an intimate relationship with our spouse is to keep our thoughts pure, because physical infidelity frequently begins with mental infidelity. Solomon warns us to not fantasize about a woman that is not our own.

> *Do not lust in your heart after her beauty or let her captivate you with her eyes.* (6:25)

> *Do not let your heart turn to her ways or stray into her paths …* (Proverbs 7:25)

Maintaining a sexually pure heart is not easy in a world that can be considered 'Temptation Island,' but the consequences of adultery are serious.

> Can a man scoop fire into his lap without his clothes being burned? Can a man walk on hot coals without his feet being scorched? So is he who sleeps with another man's wife; no one who touches her will go unpunished. (Proverbs 6:27–29)

The book of Proverbs has numerous warnings about the danger of impurity. Estes gives a clear description of purity:

> Purity is not simply a matter of external actions; it emanates from the internal motives and values of a person. … More than just satisfying one's own conscience, purity starts with a heart that sincerely desires to please the Lord. If purity is planted in the heart, then it is also culti-

---

354 For example: Proverbs 2:16–19; Proverbs 5:1–23; Proverbs 6:20–35; Proverbs 7:6–20.

vate by conduct … The conduct of a pure person is straight in at least three senses: it is a life of discipline that corresponds to God's standard, it is a life that is clearly focused on the destination of pleasing God, and it is a life that moves productively in a singular direction rather than going around in circles or meandering off God's path. Purity, then, produces conduct that remains on God's course.[355]

In his book 'The Purity War: A Biblical Guide to Living in an Immoral World, author James Cecy, suggests:

If we are going to avoid falling into the trap of immorality, we who are married must continually evaluate and improve our relationship with our spouse. Ten, twenty or thirty years from now, we can expect to live off the investment we make in our marriage today. Besides, if we don't spend time talking to our spouse about building a healthy relationship, someone else may.[356]

Avoid arguing: it is a dripping that drives our spouse away

… a quarrelsome wife is like the constant dripping of a leaky roof. (Proverbs 19:13)

Better to live on a corner of the roof than share a house with a quarrelsome wife. (Proverbs 21:9 and Proverbs 25:24)

Better to live in a desert than with a quarrelsome and nagging wife. (Proverbs 21:19)[357]

Developing and maintaining an intimate relationship with another human being is demanding work and can be challenging at times, particularly when the two of us seem to come from different planets. To deal with difference of opinion, style, preference, feeling, taste etc. can be tiring and daily arguing is around the corner.

---

[355] Estes, 252–254.

[356] Cecy, James M. *The Purity War, A Biblical guide to Living in an Immoral World.* (Condeo Press, 2011), 125.

[357] Also: "A quarrelsome wife is like the dripping of a leaky roof in a rainstorm restraining her is like restraining the wind or grasping oil with the hand." (Proverbs 27:15,16); "It is to one's honor to avoid strife, but every fool is quick to quarrel." (Proverbs 20:3)

A quarrelsome spouse[358] is compared with a *constant* dripping tap or the *constant* dripping of a leaky roof. The word 'constant' in these verses suggests that this is not about having an argument now and then with our spouse. Given the fact that spouses are usually quite different and bring different childhood (and other) experiences and personalities into the marriage, an argument now and then is inevitable. But here it refers to a constant nagging and continuing quarreling, which seems to have become a behavioral pattern of one of the spouses. One of the verses can be paraphrased as: "A nagging spouse is like the drip, drip, drip of a leaky faucet; You can't turn it off and you can't get away from it."[359] Such an attitude is foolish and can destroy a relationship and drive us apart.

No marriage lacks stressful circumstances that might cause arguing; bill needs to be paid; the neighbors are not as friendly as we would like. There might be health issues or problems related to raising children or regarding relationships with the extended family. Time and again we realize that our spouse has a totally opposite viewpoint. Nevertheless, when we *constantly* find a way to disagree with or find fault with our spouse, we are leaking the love that keeps the marriage together. Negative comments, constant fault-finding, never-ending criticism, repeatedly magnifying the spouses' flaws, day after day devaluating our spouse's efforts and accomplishments, crushes his or her spirit. The drip-drip-dripping of the nag-nag-nagging, the nit-nit-nit-picking drain-drain-drains the love and intimacy between the us and our spouse.

Express appreciation for our spouse often and publicly

Her children arise and call her blessed; her husband also, and he praises her: "Many women do noble things, but you surpass them all. Charm is deceptive, and beauty is fleeting, but a woman who fears the Lord is to be praised. Honor her for all that her hands have done and let her works bring her praise at the city gate." (Proverbs 31:28–31)

Abstaining from an argumentative attitude is important, but there is another side to the coin, namely, to develop positive words for our spouse.

It is important to consider our spouse as one of the most important people on earth that adds value to our lives. Seeing our spouse as valuable not only on

---

[358] Although the verse speaks about a wife, the same truth can equally apply to a husband.

[359] Proverbs 19:13 in Eugene Peterson's *The Message.*

our wedding day, but also after thirty-five years of marriage will go a long way in maintaining a healthy marriage that exemplifies the wisdom of God. Appreciating our spouse is one thing but seeking ways to express this appreciation verbally and publicly is an art that many of us need to learn. Verbally and publicly expressing the value of our spouse is important, not only for our spouse but also for our children. It is good for them to hear us speak with appreciation and respect about their father or mother. In the context of this chapter, it becomes clear that expressing our appreciation for our spouse goes together with 'having full confidence' in him or her (vs 11) and 'honoring' him or her (vs 31).

In chapter 31 of the book of Proverbs, the husband gives his wife full and out-loud credit for her remarkable character and her accomplishments. He does not deny that she is also physically beautiful and attractive, but he emphasizes her inner strength and her relationship with the Lord. He realized that "Like a gold ring in a pig's snout is a beautiful woman who shows no discretion" (Proverbs 11:22).

> Women tell me that the husband's opinion is what means the most to the wife. Therefore, it will mean a lot for the husband to praise his wife, to give her full credit for who she is and what she does. Accordingly, this blessed husband sings his wife a 'hallelu' (vs 28) (the verb in Hebrew 'he praises her' is that from which "Hallelu-yah" Praise ye Yahweh" comes), which is fitting, and is based on the quality of her character as shown in her lifestyle. ... Proverbs 31 teaches men that they should be quick to praise. For one thing, as a general rule, praise is the surest way to encourage healthy, good behavior in anybody. Neglecting to offer genuine praise can crush as wife's spirit. ... The man who is secure in his manhood has nothing to lose by publicly and loudly praising his wife.[360]

Build your marriage with wisdom

The wise woman builds her house, but with her own hands the foolish one tears hers down. (Proverbs 14:1)

By wisdom a house is built and through understanding it is established; through knowledge its rooms are filled with rare and beautiful treasures. (Proverbs 24:3 4)

---

[360] Phillips, 205–208.

After we have come back from our honeymoon after a beautiful wedding day, the work on our marriage is not over. On the contrary, it has just begun. Eventually, we will discover that a healthy marriage is work in progress.

If people in our societies would spend as much time on building their marriage as they spend on building, re-building, and decorating their houses, our nation's divorce rate might drop considerably.

To have healthy marriages we need wise husbands and wise wives. Being wise, that is living as God has intended it, in an intimate relationship of trust and submission with Him, has enormous consequences for the way we view our marriage and our contribution to it. Being wise means that we are a builder, while foolish behavior is compared with demolishing our house, i.e., our marriage relationship and our family.

The word 'house' in the verses above does not primarily refer to a physical building, but to 'household, marriage relationship, family.'

> The wise woman "manages her household honestly and properly and does not squander money, while the foolish woman does the opposite and thus ruins her house, that is to say, brings the husband to poverty."[361]

Cultivating a strong intimate relationship with our spouse to continuously be intoxicated with his/her love, requires discipline and wisdom. To refrain from the dripping annoyance of arguing and learn to appreciate our spouse often and publicly not only makes our marriage strong and healthy, but also reflects the wisdom of the Marriage Creator.

Questions for further reflection

1. If you are not yet married: what are you looking for in a spouse?

2. If you are married: How do you maintain a healthy marriage?

3. What is the best advice someone has given you about marriage?

---

[361] Fox, 572.

CHAPTER 11
THE WISE MAN AND HIS LIFESTYLE

The wisdom of the prudent is to discern his way
(Proverbs 14:8a)

We started our quest for wisdom by defining what we are looking for and by emphasizing that the foundation for wisdom is the fear of the LORD. We also have learned some of the basic equipment necessary for becoming wise and have identified several characteristics of being wise and how this relates to money, mouth, mates, and marriage. We have identified diligence as a crucial element in our pursuit of wisdom as well as a characteristic of the wise.

But it is important that we do not lose sight of the fact that wisdom is more than a good virtue, one among the many. Being a wise person is more than doing or saying wise things occasionally. Wisdom is a path, way of life that shapes a person into becoming wise, it is more than a one-time decision or commitment. An isolated act of wisdom does not make us into a wise person.

Wisdom is a disposition, that

> denotes the pattern of choices an individual makes. Dispositions comprise persistent attitudes or 'habits' of the heart and mind that dispose one to a consistency of certain action and expression. Bound up with perception, dispositions constitute the traits of character that are demonstrated in customary patterns of ethical behavior.[362]

Wisdom is both a gift given by God to those who fear Him, as well as a choice. A person who does not actively decide for wisdom will become a fool.

> Moral virtues are virtues of character (Greek ethos) and must be distinguished from abilities. One can possess the ability to think intelligently without have the disposition to use it. Dispositions imply a lasting 'readiness for action' formed through the agent's activity. Furthermore, moral virtues must be distinguished from 'skills for success' – sometimes called 'instrumental virtues.'[363]

---

[362] Brown William P. *Character in Crisis: A Fresh Approach to the Wisdom Literature of the Old Testament*. (Grand Rapids: Eerdmans, 1996), 9.

[363] Ibid., 10.

Once we have made a choice to become wise, we need to make sure that wisdom becomes part of our character. The qualities of wisdom that we have discussed in this book need to become our habits, which expresses itself through our conduct, or lifestyle.

This process is described well in the following rhyme:
Sow a thought, reap an act
Sow an act, reap a habit
Sow a habit, reap a character
Sow a character, reap a destiny.[364]

The book of Proverbs is one of God's instruments to help us reach our destiny. When you read the book, you get the impression that it is just a collection of interesting one-liners that are randomly put together. This might be a first impression, but it will not hold long once you begin to look more closely at this book.

One of the key metaphors that the book uses is the word 'way' or 'path'. It is a path leading to a destiny. The word 'path and its synonyms are used seventy-five times in the book of Proverbs. It refers to three things: 1) course of life (i.e., character and context of life); 2) conduct of life (i.e., specific choices and behavior); 3) consequences of that conduct (i.e., the inevitable destiny of such a lifestyle.[365]

The word 'lifestyle' might be a good current translation of it. The book of Proverbs promotes a lifestyle of wisdom, which can be described as "godliness in working clothes." (Kidner)

Reading the book of Proverbs, we can identify the following:

Behavior is path

Listen my son, accept what I say ... I instruct you in the way of wisdom and lead you along straight paths. (Proverbs 4:10)

---

[364] Based on current evidence Quote Investigator concludes that it is reasonable to attribute the words of the modern saying to Frank Outlaw, former president of Bi-Low stores in the United States, however, Quote Investigator has not yet located direct confirmation in the form of a book or interview with remarks by Outlaw. Also, the expression evolved over a long period of time. https://quoteinvestigator. com/2013/01/10/watch-your-thoughts.

[365] Waltke I, 194.

A typical person makes more than seven hundred and seventy thousand decisions during his lifetime. This is about twenty-seven choices a day – usually starting with whether to turn off the alarm or hit snooze.[366] Our lifestyle is defined by the choices we make. "Life is a matter of choices and every choice you make makes you."[367]

Our life is a journey and each choice we make is a step on that journey. When the book of Proverbs speaks about ways, paths, or walks, it refers to our patterns of conduct and our perpetual habits, our lifestyle, and the things we pursue.[368]

Our path is a habitual consistent conduct.[369] It is for this reason that we are admonished to listen, to hear, to learn, to obey, to not forget or forsake, to not despise, to not resent, and to pay attention.[370]

Every action we take leads to something, it is not an independent unit, but a building block for a way of life. When the book of Proverbs uses the metaphor 'way' and its synonyms, it refers to a behavioral pattern.

Our conduct defines our lifestyle. Our character becomes visible in our words, responses, actions, and choices. Within the book of Proverbs, we learn of the lifestyles of no less than seventeen distinct kinds of people, obviously not all of which fit the category of a lifestyle of a wise person.

There may seem to be many paths, but there are only two

The path of the righteous is like the morning sun, shining ever brighter till the full light of day. But the way of the wicked is like deep darkness; they do not know what makes them stumble. (Proverbs 4:18,19)

Although we get acquainted with seventeen different paths, or lifestyles, in the book of Proverbs[371], there are only two ways. One is called *the way, or*

---

[366] https://www.mirror.co.uk/news/uk-news/average-person-makes-773618-decisions-90742.

[367] A quote of John C. Maxwell, an American author, speaker, and pastor who has written many books, primarily focusing on leadership. https://www.passiton.com/inspirational-quotes/7735-life-is-a-matter-of-choices-and-every-choice.

[368] Proverbs 10:9; 2:8; 21:8; 15:9.

[369] Hubbard, 444.

[370] Proverbs 1:8; 3:1,11; 4:1,10,20; 5:1,7.

path, of life[372] or *the way of wisdom*[373] and the other *a way that leads to death*[374] or *the way, or path, of the wicked.*[375]

These are two highways, and each has different paths off the main road, paths that lead to the same destination. There is plurality of 'paths of life' actions and types of behavior, that all lead to life.[376]

Likewise, there are many kinds of roads off the highway to death,[377] but they end up at the same destination. It requires wisdom to recognize which path leads to which end.

The way of wisdom is presented as the way *of* life, which is also the way *to* life.[378]

> The way of wisdom is revealed to be the journey of life with wisdom as our guide, a mode of traveling through life which Yahweh approves, the foundational order of all creation and more.[379]

---

[371] Proverbs mentions: the ways of the good (2:20); the path of the upright (15:19); the path of the righteous (4:18); the course of the just (2:8); the way of God's faithful ones (2:8); paths of those that go after ill-gotten gain (1:19); paths leading to death (2:18); paths that take away life (1:19); paths, ways of the wicked (2:12; 4:14,19; 12:25; 15:9; 22:5); way of evildoers (4:14); paths, ways of the adulterous (7:25; 30:20); the way of the sluggard (15:19); ways of the violent (3:31); way of fools (12:15); way of the unfaithful (13:15); the way of the guilty (21:8); ways of the hot-tempered (21:25).

[372] Proverbs 2:19; 5:6; 10:17; 15:24.

[373] Proverbs 4:11.

[374] 2:18; 7:27; 14:12; 16:25.

[375] Proverbs 4:14.

[376] Proverbs mentions: the straight path (2:13); paths of life (2:19); paths of righteousness (2:20; 4:18); paths of justice (8:20); pleasant ways (3:17); the way of wisdom (4;11; 8:32); the way of insight (9:6); the way of the Lord (10:29); blameless ways (11;20; 28:18); a way pleasing to the Lord (16:7); the way of prudence (21:16).

[377] Proverbs mentions dark ways (2:13); crooked paths (2:15; 10:19); evil paths (28:10); perverse ways (28:6; 28:18); a path that is not good (16:29); paths that take away life (1:19), aimless paths (5:6), simple ways (1:22; 9:6); devious ways (2:15; 14:2); a way that appears to be right (14:12; 16:25).

[378] Proverbs 6:23.

[379] Habel Norman, "The Symbolism of Wisdom in Proverbs 1–9." *Interpretation: Journal of Bible and Theology* 26 (April 1972), 131–157.

Wisdom also provides us with a road map to continue this way, to consistently have a lifestyle of wisdom, avoiding the pitfalls, and potholes of the way that leads to death.

> The combination of the singular 'way' and plural 'paths' that probably branch off the main road depict life as a basic commitment with many behavioral patterns. Basically, there are only two ways: being wise or foolish, good or evil, righteous or wicked (cf 1:15). One is life; the other is death. Within that religious and ethical commitment, one makes many other ethical choices (4:26). Usually the 'way of life' is singular and the 'ways of death' is plural (7:27; 14:12). The way of live is straight, smooth, well lit, open, and public. The paths of death are crooked, rough, in deep gloom and secretive.'[380]

Every behavior has consequences

He who sows wickedness, reaps trouble ... (Proverbs 22:8)

If a man digs a pit, he will fall into it. (Proverbs 26:27)

Our behavior reveals our path, which shows our lifestyle, which as we will see defines our destiny. There is a close connection between our actions and reward or punishment. A wise person receives his rewards because of his good behavior and a foolish person receives its punishment because of his immoral behavior. This is the moral world order that is prevalent in the book of Proverbs. In the one-liners in the book of Proverbs there is often no explicit reference to God when describing this process. In several instances it formulated as an automatic process of cause and effect.[381]

Of course, this does not mean that God is not involved in this process. "God's judgment subsumes natural causality rather than the other way around."[382]

There are many references in the book of Proverbs that refer to God's involvement in the lives of people and His retribution of both good and immoral behavior.[383]

---

[380] Waltke, I, 226.

[381] For example, Proverbs 1:19; 1:31; 10:2; 10:4; 11:5,6.

[382] Fox, Michael V. *Proverbs 1–9.* (New Haven, Yale University Press, 2000), 92.

[383] For example, Proverbs 10:3,23,27; 12:2; 16:7; 19:17; 25:21,22; 28:25; 29:25,26.

In the book of Proverbs,

> no distinction is made, nor is any tension felt by the sage, between the Lord who upholds the moral order and the moral order of act-consequence itself.[384]

The principle "A man reaps what he sows" is found throughout the Bible.

In the context of Proverbs as well as the rest of the Bible is better to speak of consequences of *our behavior and character* than consequences of *our deeds.*

> Proverbs is not so mechanical as to imagine a precise correlation between every action and its result. The fool will behave in such a way that, overall, his life will be an unhappy one, but the unhappy circumstances may not be the immediate result of the one condemned in a particular proverb.[385]

God upholds these consequences, directly or indirectly.

> It is more appropriate to speak of personal divine retribution in Proverbs than of an impersonal world order. The sages believed in an taught a harmonious world worder created and sustained by the Lord, but not in impersonal one. In that world order justice will finally be meted out, but they assign that justice to the Lord without specifying the time or the manner. ... Moreover they do not assert that divine retribution operates like clockwork. ... For some people and for some times the divine retribution seems overturned. The righteous may now live in a topsy-turvy, turbulent world.[386]

As we have seen, the knowledge of this character-consequence connection is an important characteristic of a wise person.

Our lifestyle defines our destiny

Since they would not accept my advice and spurned my rebuke, they will eat the fruit of their ways and be filled with the fruit of their schemes. For the waywardness of the simple will kill them and the complacency of the fools will destroy them, but whoever listens to me will live in safety and be at ease, without fear of harm. (Proverbs 1:31–33)

---

[384] Waltke, I, 324.

[385] Fox, 91.

[386] Waltke, I, 75, 76.

The wages of the righteous is life, but the earnings of the wicked are sin and death. (Proverbs 10:16)

The faithless will be fully repaid for their ways, and the good rewarded for theirs. (Proverbs 14:14)

The path of life leads upward for the prudent to keep them from going down to the realm of the dead. (Proverbs 15:24)

Our daily choices lead to habitual conduct that develop into a lifestyle that shows our character. Our lifestyle decides our destiny. Wisdom is not just about saying the right things at the right time or knowing how to avoid an argument that could destroy a family or even a nation; or spending your money wisely.

These kinds of daily choices are part of our journey which started when we were born. The Eternal God, creator of heaven and earth and all there is, including humanity, is the Creator of life. Life is eternal. This means our journey does not stop when our body dies. Although "life after death lies beyond the horizon of Proverbs,"[387] our quest for wisdom is a desire to find our way back to the tree of life that was forfeited by our first ancestors, Adam, and Eve. They wanted wisdom without the fear of the Lord but discovered that this is the path to death.

The book of Proverbs presents us with two ways: the way of life and the way of death. It requires wisdom to recognize which path leads to which end.

> One sees ahead a confusing variety of behavioral paths. Wisdom allows one to classify each path and deduce its end point from its quality point of entry.[388]

It is important to give thought to our paths

Give careful thought to the paths for your feet and be steadfast in all your ways. (Proverbs 4:26)

The wicked put up a bold front, but the upright give thought to their ways. (Proverbs 21:29)

The wisdom of the prudent is to give thought to their ways, but the folly of fools is deception. (Proverbs 14:8)

---

[387] Kidner, 11.

[388] Fox, 130, 131.

The simple believe anything, but the prudent give thought to their steps. (Proverbs 14:15)

Whoever keeps commandments keeps their life, but whoever shows contempt for their ways will die. (Proverbs 19:16)

Knowing that our daily choices make up our lifestyle that defines our eternal destiny, it is necessary that we consider our paths. This mindset is a mark of wisdom. A wise person lives his life thoughtfully. He ponders about the ways he should go. She cares about how to life her life. Living randomly is not what human beings are supposed to do. We are not like animals, living by our instinct. We have the capacity to think, to ponder, to choose and should make full use of this creation gift, particularly when it comes to our life, one of the greatest gifts we have received from God. This means that we examine our lives regularly. Socrates said, "the unexamined life is not worth living." Understanding his ability to deceive himself, the wise person examines his life considering the truth revealed in God's Word, realizing that God examines his paths and weighs his heart and motives.[389]

> Only the omniscient, omnipotent God knows the true road that leads to life, reality as it actually is. Truth is beyond the reach of finite humanity; the Lord himself must reveal the right way through his inspired sage, and the disciple must accept that revelation by faith.[390]

A wise person is encouraged to bind God's commands and teaching on his heart, in order that

> when you walk, they will guide you; when you sleep, they will watch over you; when you awake, they will speak to you. For this command is a lamp, this teaching is a light and correction, and instruction are the way to life." (Proverbs 6:22,23)

One can change his path

At the highest point along the way, where the paths meet, she takes her stand. (8:2)

Calling out to those who pass by, who go straight on their way. (9:15)

---

[389] Proverbs 5:21; 16:2; 21:2.
[390] Waltke I, 592.

If our thoughts sow acts, that sow habits, that sow character that sow destiny, is there no way to break this automatism? Is our eternal destination fixed when we are four years old, or twelve, twenty-one fifty-three or seventy-eight? Can we not start sowing into other soil, which leads to a different harvest?[391]

Although once a person enters a path, and develops a lifestyle, he is likely to follow it to the end. It becomes his natural course and, despite its difficulties, is easier to stay on that road, than to leave. Nevertheless, during our journey of life we can experience transitional moments, encounters of various kinds, crossings that require us to choose afresh. These are forks in the road. It is at these strategic places we can hear the voice of Folly as well as the voice of Wisdom.

If we are currently walking on a way that ultimately leads to death, there is a way to get to the other highway, leading to life, when we head to invitation of Wisdom If our journey is along the path of life, we also need to continue to listen to the voice of Wisdom, and ignore the voice of Folly that can lead us astray.

Reversion: listening to woman folly

Stern discipline awaits anyone who leaves the path; the one who hates correction will die. (Proverbs 15:10)

Whoever strays from the path of prudence comes to rest in the company of the dead. (Proverbs 21:16)

Who have left the straight paths to walk in dark ways. (Proverbs 2:13)

The highway of the upright avoids evil; those who guard their ways preserve their lives. (Proverbs 16:17)

Some of the best advice can come through criticism. We have already seen that one of the characteristics of a wise person that he or she is teachable. Once we lose the willingness or ability to be corrected, we must beware. An alarm bell is beginning to ring. Heed! Heed! Do not drift away from the path of life!

---

[391] Having said this, the book of Proverbs does encourage parents to help their children from early on to develop a sensitivity for the way of wisdom. "Start children off on the way they should go, and even when they are old they will not turn from it." (22:6)

> Those who steer a straight course resolutely turn aside from evil (see
> 3:7; 14:16; 16:6), which implicitly likens the corruption and conse-
> quences of evil (see 1:16) to a condemned city with its corrupt practices
> and certain calamity (13:14–15; 15:25; 17:13). By this turning aside
> from the access roads to the condemned city, the upright stay on the
> road that is wide enough for all comers and free from all obstacles.
> Staying within the moral boundaries of this book, they walk confidently
> without fear of stumbling (4:10–19) and implicitly with the certainty of
> arriving at the final destiny.[392]

People that have developed a lifestyle of wisdom and are walking on the way
of life, should be careful to not slow down, nor begin to wander away from
the highway of life and finding themselves close to or even on the highway of
death. The wise are warned that danger lurks on the highway of death, that it
robs life; leads astray; that is detested by the Lord; that it is darkness and
leads to destruction. We are encouraged to stay away from habits, vices that
are connect to this way; to not set foot on it, to choose not to walk on it, to
not envy these ways, or turn our hearts to these.[393] The wise are encouraged
to continue listening to wisdom.[394] This will enable us to not pay attention to
the voice of folly. The book of Proverbs presents folly in a metaphor of a
woman, who call outs to people on their life's journey, to have a relationship
with her receive her gifts, which turn out to be poisonous, leading to death. All
of us meet her, as she 'sits at the door of her house, on a seat on the highest
point of the city.'[395] All of us can at time hear her call, through the media,
friends, books, films, our own hearts. We need to cherish our relationship with
woman Wisdom to not fall for the temptations of woman Folly.

Conversion: listening to woman wisdom

*She calls from the highest points of the city, "Let all who are simple come to my
house. To those who have no sense she says: Come, eat my food and drink the
wine I have mixed. Leave your simple ways and you will live. (Proverbs 9:3–6)*

*None who go to her **return** or attain the paths of life. (Proverbs 2:19)*

---

[392] Waltke, II, 26, in his comments on Proverbs 16:17.

[393] Proverbs 1:15; 3:31; 4:14,15; 22:24,25.

[394] Proverbs 1:15.

[395] Proverbs 9:14.

The book of Proverbs presents wisdom in the metaphor of a woman, who longs to give life and much more to any who want. We meet her at strategic places, such as 'the public square and noise street corners' (Proverbs 1:20,21), and 'at the highest points along the way, where the paths meet, beside the gates' (Proverbs 8:2,3) and at 'the highest points of the city' (Proverbs 9:3). It is impossible to not meet her during our journey of life.

Wisdom comes to us in a variety of ways: a thought, a comment, a book, a film, a circumstance, a friend etc. etc. Always there is an appeal, an invitation. An invitation to peace, bounty, life, joy, guidance, protection. We can ignore her appeal; we can continue our journey until her voice has been silenced. No doubt, we will meet her again, during one of the many forks in our road that we experience in life. The second time might be easier to ignore her invitation. But at one point, before it is too late, her invitation gets into your heart.

To accept her invitation, we will need to 'leave our way', to take a turn and when we do, we'll find ourselves on the way of life, which is the way of wisdom. We have found wisdom, or was it wisdom finding us? Anyhow, we discover that one of her gifts is life, *"for those who find me find life and receive favor from the Lord." (Proverbs 8:35)*

Questions for further reflection

1. Can you give an example of a good decision you made that has had enormous consequences for the rest of your life? How about a bad decision?

2. How would you describe your life in one sentence?

2. Have you had a change in lifestyle? Explain. What caused it?

CHAPTER 12
CONCLUSION:
WISDOM BETTER THAN GOLD?

Gold there is, and rubies in abundance, but lips that speak knowledge are a rare jewel. (Proverbs 20:15)

I hope that through this book I have whetted your appetite for wisdom. The world needs wise people. The business world needs wise employers and employees, and the medical world needs wise doctors and nurses. Our schools need wise teachers. Our countries need wise leaders. Our churches need wise pastors. Children need wise parents, and we need wise friends. All around us we see problems between people, communities, countries, families. Problems that cannot be solved with more money, more power, more influence. We need wisdom. All we really need can be found when we have wisdom. Repeatedly we hear that wisdom is more important than gold and jewellery. Nevertheless, as the verse above states, lips that speak knowledge, or wise words, are still rare. We have seen that wise words flow out of a wise heart and a wise heart belongs to a wise person.

Wisdom is available, but not everyone gets it. Why don't we see more of this quality in our lives, in our communities, in our families, in our world? Is it because we are not hungry enough to attain wisdom?

This seems a strange question to ask. The quest for wisdom is as old as mankind itself. As we saw in chapter one, it might be considered man's most basic drive.

But we have also seen that when our quest for wisdom is undertaken on our own, that is: in independence from our Creator, we will get stuck. In fact, we will find ourselves in opposition to Him and this will certainly mean the end of paradise. But once we begin this quest with the mindset of a formidable respect for, and submission to, the Almighty, that is a fear of Him, He will guide us along the path of wisdom, which is a path that leads to life as it is meant to be.

Wisdom and the created order

Our quest for wisdom is a desire to know reality. Reality is the divinely designed order.

> If the whole of reality comes from one wise and sovereign Lord, who has ordered all things, reality is all of one piece; nothing is independent of God, and nothing can be truly interpreted independent from God.[396]

This being the case, human beings cannot make absolute judgment claims about reality. To do so we would make ourselves God.

> If one does not make human knowledge wholly dependent upon the original self-knowledge and consequent revelation of God to man, then man will have to seek knowledge within himself as the final reference point. Then he will have to seek an exhaustive understanding of reality. He will have to hold that if he cannot attain to such an exhaustive understanding of reality, he has no true knowledge of anything at all. Either man must then know everything or he knows nothing.[397]

As we have seen, Solomon points out that wisdom is connected to the created order. God created the world by wisdom.

> *By wisdom the Lord laid the earth's foundation, by understanding he set the heavens in place; by his knowledge the deeps were divided, and the clouds let drop the dew.* (Proverbs 3:19,20)

The cosmos was made not by chance, but by God's wisdom. He brought order into chaos. If we want to be wise, i.e., to know reality, how the world works, we must navigate our lives in agreement with God's order. The world is created orderly and purposeful. God has built order in this world and through wisdom we are able to discern it and live our lives accordingly.

By wisdom a house is built, and through understanding it is established; through knowledge its rooms are filled with rare and beautiful treasures. (Proverbs 24:3,4)

In building our families, our lives, our communities, and our cultures, we need God's wisdom. Wisdom puts us in touch with the way the world is designed. This means that the wise can flourish and bring benefits to themselves and their families and communities. Being wise does not mean living our lives without stress, trouble, difficulties of suffering in several ways. The divine order is still recognizable, although the world is broken.

---

[396] Blöcher, H. "The Fear of the Lord as the 'Principle of Wisdom'" *TynBul* 28 (1977), 21.

[397] van Til C., *A Christian Theory of Knowledge* (Philadelphia: Presbyterian and Reformed, 1969), 17.

> The universe, though fractured and broken, displays the fact that its brokenness is the brokenness of order and not merely of unordered chaos. Thus it remains accessible to knowledge in part. It requires no revelation to observe the various forms of generic and teleological order which belongs to it. An unbeliever or a non-Christian culture does not have to be ignorant about the structure of the family, the virtue of mercy, the vice of cowardice, or the duty of justice. Nor does such a one have to fail entirely to respond to this knowledge in action, disposition or institution.[398]

People who do not have faith in God can live with wisdom in a practical or even ethical level, but, as we have seen in this book, finally, without the fear of God, there is no real foundation to such wisdom.

Wisdom: a gift from God or an accomplishment?

Earlier in this book we looked at the possibilities, as well as limitations, of teaching wisdom in a school. Having taken a closer look at wisdom and learned some of its key characteristics, we can ask the question whether wisdom is a gift that is divinely bestowed on us or whether it something we can acquire, using the various suggestions that are found in this book. Is wisdom imparted or developed? Is it bestowed or achieved? Is it really a quest or a request? Or is it a response to an invitation?

Based on what we have seen, it is best to conclude that it is both. Wisdom is a divine gift[399] that is acquired by anyone valuing it above everything else[400] and making a single-minded decision to accept it in humility.[401] It cannot be bought with money,[402] or acquired merely by keen observation and cogent reflection on the created order.[403] Wisdom sometimes contradicts what depraved human beings think is right.[404]

---

[398] Oliver O'Donovan, *Resurrection and the Moral Order, 88,* quoted in Tremper Longman III, The Fear of the Lord is Wisdom, 145, 146.

[399] Proverbs 2:6.

[400] Proverbs 3:13–18; 8:11,12.

[401] Proverbs 2:1–4; 3:5–8.

[402] Proverbs 17:16.

[403] Proverbs 30:1–6.

[404] Proverbs 14:12.

In her article *Ascending to Wisdom: A Christian Pedagogy*,[405]Pamela Bright,[406] looks at how wisdom was fostered in the early Christian tradition.

She comments that:

> An important aspect of the principles and practice of the Christian fostering of wisdom is the step-by-step "gradualness" of the maturing of the spiritual life.[407]

After reflecting on what Christian leaders like Benedict of Nursia, Columbanus, Augustine of Hippo, Antony of Egypt, and Francis of Assisi taught about fostering wisdom, she concludes that fostering wisdom is seen as a life-long learning process.

> This reflection on the principles and practices of fostering wisdom in the Christian tradition has underlined the fact that this pedagogy, shaped over long centuries and through diverse cultures, has neither been focused by the needs for a basic catechetical instruction, nor been oriented towards a wisdom-phase towards the end of life. It is a life-long learning process, hammered out in the ordinariness of everyday life as well as in the vertiginous landscape of mystical experience. It is a pedagogy that is adapted to both extremes and to every point in the continuum between. The examples of pedagogical practice cited ... point to the vast range of the Christian tradition of fostering wisdom, but also point to the constants in the tradition. These include the insistence on the paradoxical nature of the enterprise itself—that one is urged to acquisition of what cannot be attained except by gift. Even more paradoxical is the insistence that the inward-turning towards a seeking of self-knowledge implies a simultaneous outward-turning to the other—the neighbour in love, and to the ultimate Other, the loving one, Christ who descends to the one aspiring to ascend to wisdom.[408]

---

[405] Bright, Pamela "Ascending to Wisdom: A Christian Pedagogy" In Ferrari, Michel, and Georges Potworowski (eds.) *Teaching for Wisdom: Cross-Cultural Perspectives on Fostering Wisdom*. (New York: Springer, 2008), 163–176.

[406] Pamela Bright was professor of Historical Theology at the Concordia University in Montreal, Canada.

[407] Bright, 168.

[408] Ibid. 174–175.

Our continued quest for wisdom

Wisdom is gift that is given to those who have a desire for it, to those who have an open heart and a desire to learn. But we also have seen that wisdom is not so much a present, but it is a process. It develops in those who seek to abide by its principles. Woman Wisdom says:

> *Now then, my sons, listen to me; blessed are those who keep my ways. Listen to my instructions and be wise, do not ignore it. Blessed is the man, who listens to me, watching daily at my doors, waiting at my doorway.* (Proverbs 8:32–34)

Although we might follow a course in wisdom, we must realize that wisdom is more a walk than one step. It is not action, but attitude. Wisdom might begin with a choice, but it needs to develop into character.

> The ultimate goal of attaining wisdom is the formation of moral character.[409]

Wisdom is not just a science; it is a skill. A skill to navigate live as to be in line with the intentions and order of the Creator. Wisdom is not such much knowing, then being, or becoming, because our quest will never be fully satisfied on this side of eternity. Wisdom is not about mastering life, but about navigating life.

> Wisdom embraces the task of learning to live successfully. It involves the ability to cope with life's realities, not in the sense of dominating them, but in the sense of navigating the difficulties and assuming responsibility.[410]

Wisdom is the ability to know how to deal with the complexities of life.

The quest for wisdom is ongoing, because wisdom is not about developing a technique, but about growing a relationship. Wisdom in the book the book of Proverbs is relational.

Being wise: having a relationship with woman wisdom

In the book of Proverbs wisdom is presented to us an attractive woman. Several times Woman Wisdom speaks in the first person.[411] Wisdom is personi-

---

[409] William Brown, Character in Crisis, quoted in Bland, 13.

[410] David Bland, Proverbs and the Formation of Character, note 9, 3.

[411] For example: Proverbs 1:20–33 and Proverbs 8.

fied as a preacher with prophetic gifts, and she appears as one who makes a general appeal to humankind and strengthens her appeal by displaying her powers and the gifts which she has to offer. She refers to her closeness to God and claims she actively participated in creating the world. We might consider Woman Wisdom a personification of God's attribute of wisdom.

Tremper Longman III considers the figure of Woman Wisdom a metaphor for God's relationship with his people, alongside other metaphors, like shepherd, father, and king.

These are different manifestations of who God is for his people.[412]

When we look more closely into the identity of Woman Wisdom, we see she presents a fourfold picture of God: God acting in creation, God acting in revelation, God acting in salvation and God acting in mediation.

God acting in creation

The Lord brought me forth as the first of his works, before his deeds of old. (Proverbs 8:22)[413]

Wisdom was with God before creation of the world and humankind. Wisdom is presented as the 'architect of God's creation.'[414]

> Wisdom is regarded as closely associated with the Lord and one of his major acts – creation. In this way wisdom is given an enhanced status of supreme importance.[415]

Wisdom played an active role in creation together with God. God created the cosmos by virtue of His wisdom. Woman Wisdom claims to be the child and beloved of God, one who has observed and actively participated in the acts of

---

[412] Tremper Longman III, 33.

[413] The word qanani in verse 22 caused much debate among scholars. This debate is about whether this word means "God acquired (or possessed) me" or "created me," "brought me forth."

[414] Proverbs 8:30. Scholars are debating the meaning of the word *amon* in Proverbs 8:30. The issue is whether this word means 'a master craftsman or architect', who actively participated in God's creation of the world, or whether the word should be interpreted as 'brought up', referring to wisdom as having been a little child at the time of the creation of the world, which would exclude the notion that she participated actively in the work of creation.

[415] Boström, 51.

creation. She makes this claim to show her primordial origin and her closeness to God. She says she "always rejoices in the presence of God."[416] Also this mutual knowledge of knowing God and being known by God is highlighted.[417]

God acting in revelation

Woman Wisdom actively seeks men rather than being there to be sought. The whole emphasis is on the initiative of God in revealing Himself as Wisdom and, combined with the relating of 'the fear of the Lord' to everyday life.

> The term Wisdom is significant for our thinking about God and especially his relationship with men, that is, as a medium of revelation.[418]

The fact that Woman Wisdom is the "firstborn," emphasizes that no one can afford to not listen to her (Proverbs 8:32) to her, in view of her close association with God.

> Referring to her old age, a very special quality, that gives her a smell of godliness, wisdom commends itself to humanity. Wisdom legitimizes herself and she bases this on her being created by God before all times."[419]

Wisdom is personified as a preacher with prophetic gifts. She is bold. We find her in the streets, the squares, the city gates.[420] She shouts out from the hilltop near the road and at the crossroads.[421]

Wisdom sends messengers.[422] When Woman Wisdom cries aloud in the streets and public places and appeals to man, she does not point to someone or something else, but puts herself at centre of all the good things she has to offer.

> The most important thing is that wisdom does not turn towards man in the shape of an "It" teaching, guidance, salvation or the like, but in the

---

[416] Proverbs 8:30.

[417] Proverbs 8:12.

[418] Jones, Edgar. *Proverbs and Ecclesiastes: Introduction and Commentary* (London: SCM Press, 1961), 43, 44.

[419] Tuinstra, E.W. *Spreuken I* [Proverbs 1] (Baarn: Callenbach, 1996), 203.

[420] Proverbs 1:20–33.

[421] Proverbs 8:1,2.

[422] Proverbs 9:3.

> shape of a person, a summoning "I." So wisdom is truly the form in which Yahweh makes Himself present and in which he wishes to be sought by man.[423]

> Wisdom speaks in her own person with her own authority. The intention is to encourage the pupil to cleave to her, to develop a personal relationship with her.[424]

God acting in salvation

Wisdom is seen as sharing in the process of creation and in the redemption of that creation. God is Creator and Redeemer, and these activities are linked with Wisdom. They emphasize the choice between life and death. Wisdom possesses the authority to boldly claim: "He who finds me finds life and obtains favour from God." (Proverbs 8:35) This is a remarkable statement and expresses the close relationship between God and Woman Wisdom, because only God can speak in this way.

> The kerygma of wisdom can be summed up in one word: life.[425]

The concept of 'life' as found in the book of Proverbs, is quite elastic. It can refer to a long life: sheer existence in many days.[426] It can refer to a harmonious family life[427] and even of vitality of one's whole being.[428] But in several places, it is not too much to say that 'life' means fellowship with God.

> This understanding of 'life' as implying more than mere existence is expressed most tellingly in the phrases 'tree of life', 'fountain of life' and 'path' or 'way of life'.[429]

Tree and fountain of life refer to God's sources of renewal, temporal and spiritual, and symbolize the blessings of a right relationship to God.

---

423 Murphy, 13.

424 Dermot Cox, O.F.M. *Proverbs with an Introduction to Sapiential Books* (Wilmington Delaware: Michael Glazier Inc, 1982), 158.

425 Murphy, 9.

426 Proverbs 3:2,16; 4:10; 9:11.

427 Proverbs 15:27.

428 Proverbs 3:22.

429 Kidner, 54.

> The metaphors tell their own story, but this is reinforced by the overtones of Genesis 2 and 3, where the tree bore the fruit of immortality, ...[430]

Although here and there Proverbs provides a glimpse of viewing life as a goal beyond the grave,[431] life after death, as we now understand it, lies beyond the horizon of Proverbs.

Nevertheless, in the book of Proverbs:

Life was a great grace – it was all, and it depended upon one's relationship to the living God.[432]

In Proverbs 1:24–32, Woman Wisdom makes clear what the consequences are for rejecting her and her message. The call of Woman Wisdom to make a choice and the contrast with foolishness, underlines the seriousness of her message. It is a choice between life and death.[433]

Wisdom is associated with righteousness (8:6), truth (8:7), wholesome behaviour (8:8) and good judgment (8:12), with common sense, success, insight, and strength (8:14,15). On the other hand, she tells us that she stays as far away as possible from deception, evil, pride, and arrogance (8:7,8,13).

God acting in mediation

In looking at Woman Wisdom, it is important to not only focus on her relationship with God, but also her relationship with and function in the world of human beings. She claims to have "rejoiced in his (God's) created world and delighted in mankind."[434] The picture given of Woman Wisdom is that of a mediator between God and man.

> The arrangement in verses 30, 31 clearly shows that there is a dual relationship between (1) wisdom and the Lord, on the one hand, and (2) wisdom and creation and mankind on the other. Wisdom plays before the Lord and is his delight, but she also plays on his earth, the abode of

---

[430] Ibid.

[431] e.g., Proverbs 11:7; 12:28; 14:32).

[432] Murphy, 13.

[433] Proverbs 1:20–33; 8:2–21; 9:1–6.

[434] Proverbs 8:30,31.

mankind, and her delight is mankind. In a sense, wisdom functions as an intermediary between God and man, between God and his world.[435]

The personified Wisdom in Proverbs 1–9 is a poetical device employed by the wise to express that wisdom was a mediator of the godly presence, as a means of bringing God and man together.[436]

Central to a proper understanding of the phenomenon of personification of wisdom is the fact of an abstract name being used. Yahweh is himself wise, and he desires a relationship to man, so His wisdom becomes a dynamic of relationship, and so a person. The personification emphasizes the desirability of wisdom, something that is so personal it must be acquired if one seeks life. Wisdom thus becomes a force in which God makes himself present and in which he wishes to be sought. Prov. 8:35 shows Wisdom speaking as if she were God. Wisdom is a channel by which God can reach out to humanity, and draw humanity to himself.[437]

Woman Wisdom is presented as an agent of creation that has an intimate relationship with God before the creation of the world; and as a medium of revelation of the true and only God, who actively seeks the wellbeing of men, and who boldly declares to be the centre of salvation, offering nothing less than life itself and thereby carrying out the role of mediator between God and man.

When contemplating on the place that Woman Wisdom receives in the Book of Proverbs, as a way of asserting God's nearness, his involvement in His world and his concern for His people, as a reverential synonym for God, as a perfect description of the immanence of God, the reaching out of the exalted God which the wise man experiences here on earth, that which man may know of God and of God's will, it is no wonder that the first Christians identified Christ as Wisdom and that in the New Testament Jesus is presented as the incarnation of God's wisdom.

The early Church Fathers looked upon the sublime personification of wisdom in chapter 8 as one of the clearest pictures of Christ in the Old

---

[435] Boström, 55.

[436] Tuinstra, 28.

[437] Dermot Cox, 74.

Testament, and in many instances they used this passage to help formulate their ideas about the Second Person of the Trinity.[438]

May the only wise God,
who in the person of Jesus Christ
made His eternal wisdom become flesh and blood,
and who in the person of the Holy Spirit,
who is called the Spirit of Wisdom,
bless you and fill you with His wisdom
and help us to make His wisdom our own.
Amen.

Questions for further reflection

1. What is the main lesson you have learned from reading this book?

2. What specific steps are you going to take to grow in wisdom?

3. Whom of your friends would also benefit from this book? Why? How are you going to introduce the content of this book to him or her?

---

[438] Fritsch, Charles T. "The Gospel in the Book of Proverbs." *Theology Today*, April, 1950, 170.

APPENDIX
BACKGROUND INFORMATION
ABOUT THE BOOK OF PROVERBS

In this book we have been looking at various aspects of wisdom as it is presented to us in the book of Proverbs. It might help us to have some background information about this book in the Bible.

One of the first things that we notice when we start reading the book of Proverbs is that it is different from most other books in the Bible. There are no references to historical accounts and traditions related to the people of Israel like those of the patriarchal narratives, the Exodus, Sinai, the law or the covenant. The bulk of the proverbs in the book of Proverbs do not seem to have any specific reference to the religious life in Israel. The book does not speak of the tabernacle, temple or priesthood. The number of references in the book to acts of worship – sacrifice, the making of vows and prayer – is very small. The book is silent about the various kings both in Israel and beyond. We do hear nothing of prophets, who pass on words of judgment or salvation when they say: 'so speaks the Lord ...". This lack of references to history seems to be intentional to express truths and deal with problems that are timeless and common to all peoples.

In the book of Proverbs, we become aware of our fellow men as human beings rather than as Israelites or Gentiles. The book emphasizes that God is broader than worship, ethics, evangelism and eschatology, and has a voice in sociology, education, art and science.

The sayings in the book of Proverbs focus on individuals and on their concerns without restriction to specific national affiliations. They are applicable to all people at any period in history and in this sense may be characterized as universalistic. In the book of Proverbs, we meet one hundred-eighty different kinds of people, including forty-three kinds of men and twenty-three kinds of women.

Salomon: the author and editor

The book begins with the words: "The proverbs of Solomon, son of David, king of Israel" (1:1) and also in chapter 10:1 we read: "The proverbs of Solomon."

Solomon lived from 971 till 931 B.C. and was king of Israel most of his life. Shortly after he succeeded his father David as king, God appeared to him in a dream and asked him: "Ask, what I shall give you." (1 Kings 3:5). Solomon asked for wisdom so that he could govern God's people and discern between good and evil. (1 Kings 3:9). God was pleased with this answer and made him one of the wisest people on earth.

Some of the wisdom that Solomon received from God is found in the book of Proverbs. Because Solomon spoke 3,000 proverbs, his proverbs found in the book of Proverbs are only a fraction of his total repertoire. A careful reading of the book shows that not all the text is directly from Solomon. Solomon is the author of chapters 1–22. Chapter 25–29 are proverbs of Solomon collected by the men of Hezekiah (chapter 25–29), after Solomon's death. We also read about 'the sayings of the wise' (22:17; 24:23), the sayings of Agur, son of Jakeh, king of Massa (30:1) and 'the sayings of King Lemuel, king of Massa' (31:1). This means that Solomon included wisdom sayings of surrounding nations in the book of Proverbs, which he believed were in harmony with the truth of God.

The readers and purpose

According to the introduction of the book (1:1–7), the book of Proverbs particularly addresses immature young men, with the purpose of making them wise, providing them with insight, knowledge and discretion in order to live justly and righteously.

Style

The book of Proverbs is a poetic book, using several different forms of Hebrew poetry.

The wisdom in this book is presented in two ways:

1. In chapters 1 to 9 we find instructions: long poems where someone is addressed who needs to learn some basic life skills; it often is a younger person, who is addressed as 'son'. The speaker is a father figure or wisdom teacher. Here and there Wisdom is being presented as a person. These chapters are essentially an essay about wisdom.

2. In chapters 10–31 wisdom is being presented through proverbs, pity sayings of usually two sentences. The book of Proverbs consists of about five hundred of such proverbs.

The Hebrew word for proverb is 'masal' which means 'comparison', 'parable' 'analogy', or 'a brief, pithy saying.'

The book contains a lot of imagery or figurative language, including one-liners, brief, sometimes humorous sayings, stating truth using only a few words. We might call the book of Proverbs a collection of short sentences based on long experiences.

In the book we find several characteristic forms of Hebrew poetry, such as: rhetorical questions;[439] beatitudes – pointing to a state of well-being;[440] comparative sayings – pointing to two subjects, often dissimilar at first appearance, that are said to resemble each other in some way;[441] numerical proverbs – a literary form to express that there are a number of different examples of a given phenomenon, but that only a few are mentioned;[442] alphabet acrostic poem – each sentence begins with a consecutive letter of the Hebrew alphabet.[443]

Parallelism is the poetic form found most in the book of Proverbs. This form is called 'parallelism' because it contains two lines that run parallel to each other. In the book of Proverbs, we can identify several types of parallelism:

- synonymous parallelism, whereby the two lines say the same thing, but use different words, e.g. How much better to get wisdom than gold, to get insight rather than silver (16:16).

- *synthetic parallelism*, whereby the second line, sharpens and intensifies the thought of the first line. For example: *Even in laughter the heart may ache, and joy may end in grief (14:13).*

- antithetical parallelism, whereby the second line presents the same truth as the first line, but from an opposite perspective. For example: The wise woman builds her house, but with her own hands the foolish one tears hers down (14:1).

- comparative parallelism, whereby the two lines are compared to each other with words, 'like' … For example: Like an earring of gold or an ornament of silver, is a wise man's rebuke to a listening ear (25:12).

---

439 For example: Proverbs 20:9,24; 22:27.

440 For example: Proverbs 8:33,34; 14:21; 16:20; 29:18.

441 For example: Proverbs 10:26; 11:22; 19:12; 20:2; 25:3,13,14; 26:7–11.

442 For example: Proverbs 6:16–19; 30:15,16,18,19,21–23.

443 For example: Proverbs 31:10–31.

- *Better-than parallelism,* whereby the two lines are compared to each other and the truth/behaviour/situation in first line is better than the truth/behaviour/situation in the second line. For example: *Better a little with the fear of the Lord than great wealth with turmoil. (15:16)*

The book of Proverbs: handle with care!

When reading the book of Proverbs we need to keep in mind that the proverbs are situation sensitive. A proverb is not always and, in every circumstance, true, but presupposes the right circumstance for its proper application. Because most proverbs use figurative language, they are not always precise and that they cannot always be taken literally. Proverbs state truth in a condensed way, worded such that it is easy to remember.

As with the rest of scripture we need to understand the verses of Proverbs within the context in which they appear in the book and within the context of the whole of the Bible. Often it is not so easy to understand the context of the isolated proverbs in the book of Proverbs as they seem to be randomly put next to one another. Nevertheless, it is important to compare what we read in a proverb with the truths of other proverbs and of what God has revealed elsewhere in His Word. Many proverbs state truths that made sense in the time of Solomon, but they need to be adapted to our times. It is also important to realize that the proverbs cannot be taken as promises of God that will always become true, but they must be understood as general guidelines for living a successful life.

Is there a story line in the book of Proverbs?

We have seen that the book of Proverbs is written with a clear goal. Nevertheless, when you read the chapters of this book it often seems like a hodgepodge. The verses seem to have been put together in a random way and it is hard to find a coherent story. Sometimes it seems several consecutive verses address the same topic and of course in the first nine chapters of the book we find longer discourses, but overall, each verse seems to stand on its own. Several theologians have tried hard to find a certain systematic structure in the book, while others have given up because they could not come to a clear conclusion. The book of Proverbs therefore reflects human life, which most often also lacks order and structure.

As we have seen, the focus of the book is to encourage the reader/listener to become a wise person. Around this focus a beautiful garden has been built, in which we can find a variety of plants (the verses). Here and there we discover a path that connects the flower beds, but overall, we must conclude that each flower has its own worth and deserves our attention and wants to share her smell and color with us. In this book I have put together a bouquet of these flowers to help you grow in becoming a wise man or woman.

BIBLIOGRAPHY

Abdullah, Abdul Hakim & Kabara Auwal Halabi "The Wisdom: A Concept of Character Building Based on Islamic View." *International Journal of Academic Research in Business and Social Sciences* 2017, Vol. 7, No. 5.

Alford, Henry. *Alford's Greek Testament: An Exegetical and Critical Commentary*. (Bellingham, WA: Logos Research Systems Inc., 2010).

Anders, Max. *Proverbs.* Holman Old Testament Commentary, (Nashville, Tennessee: Broadman and Holman Publishers, 2005).

Ardelt, Monica. "Empirical Assessment of a Three-Dimensional Wisdom Scale." *Research on Aging*, Vol. 25 No. 3, May 2003.

Ardelt, M. "Where can wisdom be found: A Reply to the Commentaries by Baltes and Kunzmann, Sternberg, and Achenbaum." *Human Development* 2004.

Ardelt, M. "Being wise at any age." In Shane J. Lopez (Ed.): *Positive psychology: Exploring the best in people. Volume 1: Discovering human strengths* (Westport, CT: Praeger, 2008).

Ardelt, Monika. "The development of wisdom across the life span: A re-examination of an ancient topic." In P.B. Baltes & O.G. Brim, Jr. (Eds.), *Life-span development and behavior* Vol. 3. (San Diego, CA: Academic Press, 1980).

Baltes, Paul B. *Wisdom as Orchestration of Mind and Virtue*, Max Planck Institute for Human Development, Berlin Book in preparation, 2004.

Baltes P. B, Smith J, Staudinger UM. "Wisdom and successful aging." 123–167 in Sonderegger (Ed), *Psychology and Aging*; Nebraska Symposium on Motivation, 1991.

Baltes P.B. & Smith, J. (1990b). "Towards a psychology of wisdom and its ontogenesis." In R.J. Sternberg (Ed.), *Wisdom – Its nature, origins, and development*, 87–120) (Cambridge, UK: Cambridge University Press, 1990).

Baltes, P.B. & Staudinger, U. (2000). "Wisdom: A metaheuristic (pragmatic) to orchestrate mind and virtue toward excellence." *American Psychologist*, 55(1).

Bartholomew, Craig G., and Ryan P. O'Dowd. *Old Testament Wisdom Literature: A Theological Introduction*. (Downers Grove, Ill.: IVP Academic,2011).

Bland, Dave. *Proverbs and the Formation of Character*. (Eugene, Oregon: Cascade Books, 2015).

Blöcher, H. "The Fear of the Lord as the 'Principle of Wisdom'" *TynBul 28* (1977).

Boström, L. *The God of the Sages: The Portrayal of God in the Book of Proverbs*. (Stockholm: Almqvist & Wiksell, 1990).

Bridges, Jerry. *The Joy of Fearing God*. (Colorado: Waterbrook Press, 1997).

Brown William P. *Character in Crisis: A Fresh Approach to the Wisdom Literature of the Old Testament*. (Grand Rapids: Eerdmans, 1996).

Brown, S. C. "Learning across the campus: How college facilitates the development of wisdom". *Journal of College Student Development*, 45(2), 2004.

Brown SC, Greene JA. "The Wisdom Development Scale: translating the conceptual to the concrete." *Journal of College Student Development*. 2008.

Cecy, James M. *The Purity War, A Biblical guide to Living in an Immoral World*. (Condeo Press, 2011).

Clinton, Robert J. *Strategic Concepts that Clarify a Focused Life*. (Altadena, CA: Barnabas Publishers, 2005).

Crenshaw, James L. *Old Testament Wisdom; An Introduction*. (London: SCM Press Ltd, 1982).

Curtis, Edward M., John J. Brugaletta, *Discovering the Way of Wisdom*. (Grand Rapids: Kregel Publications, 2004).

Dermot Cox, O.F.M. *Proverbs with an Introduction to Sapiential Books* (Wilmington Delaware: Michael Glazier Inc, 1982).

Estes, Daniel J. *Handbook on the Wisdom books and Psalms*. (Grand Rapids, Michigan: Baker Academic, 2005).

Ferrari, Michel, and Georges Potworowski (eds.) *Teaching for Wisdom: Cross-Cultural Perspectives on Fostering Wisdom*. (New York: Springer, 2008).

Field, Claud, *Wisdom of the East, the Confessions of Al Ghazzali: Translated for the First Time into English*. (London: Forgotten Books, 2008).

Fox, Michael V. *Proverbs 1–9*. (New Haven, Yale University Press, 2000).

Fritsch, Charles T. "The Gospel in the Book of Proverbs." *Theology Today*, April, 1950.

Frydrych, Thomas. *Living Under the Sun: Examination of Proverbs and Qoheleth*. (Boston: Brill, 2002).

Goleman, Daniel Goleman. *Emotional Intelligence*. (New York: BantamBooks, 1995).

Habel, Norman, "The Symbolism of Wisdom in Proverbs 1–9." *Interpretation: Journal of Bible and Theology 26* (April 1972).

Hassell Bullock, C. *An Introduction to the Old Testament Poetic Books*. (Chicago: Moody, 1988).

Hubbard, David A. *Proverbs*. The Preacher's Commentary Series, Volume 15. (Nashville: Nelson, 1989).

Ironside, H.A. *Proverbs*. (Neptune, New Jersey: Loizeaux Brothers, 1996) .

Jeste, Dilip V. Jeste, Monika Ardelt, Dan Blazer, Helena C. Kraemer, George Vaillant, and Thomas W. Meeks "Expert Consensus on Characteristics of Wisdom: A Delphi Method Study" *The Gerontologist* Vol. 50, No. 5.

Jones, Edgar Jones. *Proverbs and Ecclesiastes: Introduction and Commentary* (London: SCM Press, 1961).

Kidner, Derek. *Proverbs*. Tyndale Old Testament Commentaries, (Nottingham: InterVarsity Press, 2008).

Kidner, Derek. *Ezra & Nehemiah* (Downers Grove: InterVarsity Press, 1979).

Kowalczyk, Stanislaw. "Topicality of St. Augustine's Concept of Wisdom" *Dialogue and Universalism*, Volume 16, Issue 5/6, 2006.

Van Leeuwen, Raymond. "Building God's House – an exploration in Wisdom" – In *The way of wisdom: Essay in Honor of Bruce K. Waltke* J.I. Packer, Sven K. Soderlund (eds) (Grand Rapids, Michigan: Zondervan Publishing House, 2000).

Le Gai Eaton, Charles. *Islam and the Destiny of Man* (Albany: SUNY, 1986).

Lopez, Shane J. (Ed.). *Positive psychology: Exploring the best in people. Volume 1: Discovering human strengths*. (Westport, CT: Praeger, 2008.)

MacDonald, Gordon. *When Men Think Private Thoughts*. (Nashville, Tennessee: Thomas Nelson Inc., 1997) .

MacDonald, Gordon. *Ordering your Private World*. (Nashville: Thomas Nelson Publishers, 1985).

Masami, Takahashi & Prashant Bordia." The Concept of Wisdom: A Cross-cultural Comparison." *International Journal of Psychology*, 2000 35:1.

McGinnis, Alan Loy. *The Friendship Factor: how to get closer to the people you care for*. (Minneapolis: Augsburg Publishing House, 1979).

McKane, William. *Proverbs.* Old Testament Library. (Philadelphia: Westminster, 1970).

Murray, John. *Principles of Conduct* (Grand Rapids, Eerdmans, 1957).

Oosterhoff, B.J. *De Vreze des HEREN in het Oude Testament.* (Utrecht: Kemink en Zoon, 1949).

Origin. *On First Principles.* (Notre Dame IN: Ave Maria Press Inc., 2013).

Outliers, Gladwell M. *The Story of Success.* (San Francisco: Little, Brown and Company, 2008).

Packer, J.I. *Knowing God,* (London: Hodder and Stoughton, 2013).

Packer, J.I. and Sven K. Soderlund (eds). *The way of wisdom: Essay in Honor of Bruce K. Waltke* (Grand Rapids, Michigan: Zondervan Publishing House, 2000).

Peterson, Eugene H. *A Long Obedience in the Same Direction* (Downers Grove, Ill: InterVarsity, 1980).

Phillips, Dan. *God's Wisdom in Proverbs, Hearing God's voice in Scripture.* (The Woodlands: Kress Biblical Resources, 2011).

von Rad, Gerard. *Wisdom in Israel.* (London: SCM Press, 1972).

Ross, Allan P. "Proverbs" in *The Expositor's Bible Commentary, Proverbs-Isaiah*, Vol. 6 Tremper Longman III and David E. Garland (eds.) (Grand Rapids, Michigan: Zondervan, 2008).

Sanders, Oswald. *Spiritual Leadership.* (Chicago: Moody Press, 1994).

Sandoval, Timothy J., *The Discourse of Wealth and Poverty in the Book of Proverbs,* Leiden: Brill, 2006).

Sinclair, Maurice W. *Pathways of Wisdom: Human philosophies and the purpose of God* (Nottingham: Apollos, 2010).

Smally, Gary & John Trent, *The Language of Love: How to Quickly Communicate your Feelings and Needs.* (Wheaton, Illinois, Tyndale House Publishers, 1988).

Stanley, Charles. *Walking Wisely.* (Nashville, Tennessee: Thomas Nelson, 2002).

Sternberg, Robert J. *Why Smart People Can be so Stupid* (New Haven: Yale University Press, 2003).

Sternberg, Robert J. "A balance theory of wisdom." *Review of General Psychology*, 1998, 2(4) .

Sternberg, R.J. (Ed.), *Wisdom – Its nature, origins, and development.* (Cambridge, UK: Cambridge University Press,1990).

Sternberg, Robert J. "How Wise Is It to Teach for Wisdom? A Reply to Five Critiques." *Educational Psychologist*, 2001, 36:4.

Strong, James. *Strong's Exhaustive Concordance of the Bible.* (Peabody, Massachusetts: Hendrickson Publishers, 2007).

Swanson, Kevin. *The Book of Proverbs: God's Book of Wisdom Book 1.* (Elizabeth, CO: Generations with Vision, 2011).

Swidler, Leonard. "A Christian Historical Perspective on Wisdom" *Journal of Ecumenical Studies,* 33:4, Fall 1996.

Swindoll, Charles. R. *Active Spirituality.* (Milton Keynes, Nelson Word Ltd., 1994).

Targowski, Andrew. WISDOM HNRS 4900-Spring 2012; (Kalamazoo, MI: A. Targowski/Civilization Press, 2012).

van Til, C. *A Christian Theory of Knowledge.* (Philadelphia: Presbyterian and Reformed, 1969).

Toombs, Lawrence E. Toombs. "O.T. Theology and the Wisdom Literature" *Journal of Bible and Religion* 23 (1952).

Tozer, A.W. *The Knowledge of the Holy.* (San Francisco: Harper and Row, Publishers, 1961).

Tremper Longman III, *How to Read Proverbs.* (Downers Grove: InterVarsity Press, 2002).

Tremper Longman III, *The Fear of the Lord is Wisdom*, (Grand Rapids, Michigan: Baker Academic, 2017).

Tremper Longman III, *Proverbs.* Baker Commentary on the Old Testament Wisdom and Psalms. (Grand Rapids MI: Baker Academic, 2006).

Tremper Longman III and David E. Garland (eds.), *The Expositor's Bible Commentary, Proverbs-Isaiah, Vol. 6* (Grand Rapids, Michigan: Zondervan, 2008).

Trowbridge, Richard Hawley, "The Scientific Approach of Wisdom", doctoral dissertation (Union Institute & University Cincinnati, Ohio, 2005).

Waltke, Bruce K. *The Book of Proverbs: Chapters 1–15.* New International Commentary on the Old Testament Series. (Grand Rapids, Mich. and Cambridge, UK: William B. Eerdmans Publishing Co. 2004).

Waltke, Bruce K. *The Book of Proverbs: Chapters 15–31*. New International Commentary on the Old Testament Series. (Grand Rapids, Mich. and Cambridge, UK: William B. Eerdmans Publishing Co. 2005).

Waltke, Bruce. "The Book of Proverbs and Ancient Wisdom Literature", *Bibliotheca Sacra* 136 (1979).

Whybray, R.N. *Wisdom in Proverbs* (London: S. C. M., 1965).

Whybray, R.N. *The Book of Proverbs: A Survey of Modern Study*. HBIS 1. (Leiden: Brill.1995).

Wilson, William. *Wilson's Old Testament Word Studies*. (Peabody, Massachusetts: Hendrickson Publishers, 1990).

Woodcock, Eldon; *Proverbs, A Topical Study*. (Grand Rapids, Michigan: Zondervan, 2001).

Young, Robert. *Young's Analytical Concordance to the Bible*. (Illinois: Tyndale House Publishers House, 1984)

Zuck, Roy B. "A Theology of the Wisdom Books and the Song of Songs", in *A Biblical* Theology *of the Old Testament* (Zuck, ed.) (Chicago: Moody Publishers, 1991).